ISBN 978-1-330-59392-9
PIBN 10062127

1 MONTH OF
FREE
READING

at

www.ForgottenBooks.com

By purchasing this book you are eligible for one month membership to ForgottenBooks.com, giving you unlimited access to our entire collection of over 700,000 titles via our web site and mobile apps.

To claim your free month visit:

www.forgottenbooks.com/free62127

English
Français
Deutsche
Italiano
Español
Português

www.forgottenbooks.com

Mythology Photography **Fiction**
Fishing Christianity **Art** Cooking
Essays Buddhism Freemasonry
Medicine **Biology** Music **Ancient
Egypt** Evolution Carpentry Physics
Dance Geology **Mathematics** Fitness
Shakespeare **Folklore** Yoga Marketing
Confidence Immortality Biographies
Poetry **Psychology** Witchcraft
Electronics Chemistry History **Law**
Accounting **Philosophy** Anthropology
Alchemy Drama Quantum Mechanics
Atheism Sexual Health **Ancient History**
Entrepreneurship Languages Sport
Paleontology Needlework Islam
Metaphysics Investment Archaeology
Parenting Statistics Criminology
Motivational

NUGÆ,

BY NUGATOR;

OR,

Pieces in Prose and Verse.

BY ST. LEGER L. CARTER.

BALTIMORE:

PRINTED BY WOODS AND CRANE.

1844.

-

CONTENTS.

NUGÆ.

MARCH COURT.

COURT DAY! what an important day in Virginia! what a day of bustle and business! what a requisition is made upon every mode of conveyance to the little metropolis of the County! How many debts are then to be paid!—how many to be put off! Alas! how preponderate the latter! If a man says, "I will pay you at Court," I give up the debt as hopeless, without the intervention of the *la*. But if Court day be thus important, how much more so is March Court! That is the day when our candidates are expected home from Richmond, to give an account of their stewardship; at least it used to be so, before the number of our legislators was lessened, with a view of facilitating the transaction of business, and with a promise of shortening the sessions. But, somehow or other, the public chest has such a multitude of charms, it seems now to be more impossible than ever to get away from it.

> " 'Tis that capitol rising in grandeur on high,
> Where bank notes, by thousands, bewitchingly lie,"

as the song says, which makes our sessions "of so long a life;" and there is no practicable mode of preventing the evisceration of the aforesaid chest, but deferring the meeting of the Assembly to the month of February, and thereby compelling the performance of the commonwealth's business within the two months which would intervene 'till the planting of corn. However, this is foreign to my present purpose, which is to describe a scene at which I have often gazed with infinite amusement. Would I had the power of Hogarth, that I might perpetuate the actings and doings of a March Court; but having no turn that way, I must barely attempt to group the materials, and leave the painting to some regular artist to perfect.

2

Picture to yourself, my gentle reader, our little town of Dumplingsburg, consisting of a store, a tavern, and a blacksmith shop, the common constituents of a county town, with a court house and a jail in the foreground, as denoting the superior respect to which they are entitled. Imagine a number of roads diverging from the town, like the radii of a circle, and upon these roads horsemen and footmen of every imaginable kind, moving, helter skelter, to a single point of attraction. Justices and jurymen—counsellors and clients—planters and pettifoggers—constables and cake-women—farmers and felons—horse-drovers and horse-jockies, all rushing onward like the logs and rubbish upon the current of some mighty river, swollen by rains, hurrying pell mell to the vast ocean which is to swallow them all up—a simile not altogether unapt, when we consider that the greater part of these people have law business, and the law is universally allowed to be a vortex worse than the Maelstrom. Direct the "fringed curtains of thine eyes" a little further to the main street—a street well entitled to the epithet main, in all its significations, being, in truth, the principal and only street, and being, moreover, the political arena or cockpit, in which are settled, pugilistically, all the tough and knotty points which cannot be adjusted by argument. See, on either side, rows of nags of all sorts and sizes, from the skeleton just unhitched from the plough, to the saucy, fat, impudent pony, with roached mane and bobtail, and the sleek and long-tailed pampered horse, whose coat proclaims his breeding, all tied to the staggering fence which constitutes the boundary of the street. Behold the motley assemblage within these limits, hurrying to and fro with rapid strides, as if life were at stake. Who is he who slips about among the "greasy rogues," with outstretched palm, and shaking as many hands as the Marquis Lafayette? It is the candidate for election, and he distributes with liberal hand that barren chrouicle of legislative deeds, demominated the list of laws, upon which are fed a people starving for information. This is a mere register of the titles of acts passed at the last session, but it is caught at with avidity by the sovereigns, who are highly offended if they do not come in for a share of the delegate's bounty. The purchase and distribution of these papers is a sort of *carmen necessarium,* or indispensable lesson, and it frequently happens that a member of the Assembly who has been absent from his post the whole winter, except upon the yeas and nays, acquires credit for his industry and attention to business, in proportion to the magnitude of the bundle he distributes of this uninstructive record.

See, now he mounts some elevated stand, and harangues the gaping crowd, while a jackass, led by his groom, is braying at the top of his lungs just behind him. The jack takes in his breath, like Fay's snorer, "with the tone of an octave flute, and lets it out with the profound depth of a trombone." Wherever a candidate is seen, there is sure to be a jackass; surely his long-eared companion does not mean to satirize the candidate! However that may be, you perceive the orator is obliged to desist, overwhelmed, perhaps, by this thundering applause. Now the crowd opens to the right and left, to make way for some superb animal at full trot, some Highflyer or Daredevil, who is thus exhibited *ad captandum vulgus,* which seems the common purpose of the candidate, the jack, and his more noble competitor. But look, here approaches an object more terrible than all, if we may judge from the dispersion of the crowd, who ensconce themselves behind every convenient corner, and peep from their lurking holes, while the object of their dread moves onward, with saddle-bags on arm, a pen behind his ear, and an inkhorn at his button-hole. Lest some of my readers should be ignorant of this august personage, I must do as they do in England, where they take a shaggy dog, and dipping him in red paint, they dash him against the sign board, and write underneath, this is the Red Lion. This is the sheriff, and he is summoning his jury. "Mr. Buckskin, you, sir, dodging behind the blacksmith's shop, I summon you on the jury;" ah, luckless wight! he is caught and obliged to succumb. In vain he begs to be let off, "you must apply to the magistrates," is the surly reply. And if, reader, you could listen to what passes afterwards in the court house, you might hear something like the following colloquy :

Judge. "What is your excuse, sir ?"

Juror. "I am a lawyer, sir."

Judge. "Do you follow the law now, sir ?"

Juror. "No, sir, the law follows me."

Judge. "Swear him, Mr. Clerk."

Ah, there is a battle ! ! ! see how the crowd rushes to the spot,—"who fights ?"—"part 'em"—"stand off"—"fair play"—"let no man touch"—"hurrah, Dick"—"at him, Tom." An Englishman, thinking himself in England, bawls out, "Sheriff! read the riot act!" A justice comes up and commands the peace ; *inter arma silent leges ;* he is unceremoniously knocked down, and justice is blind, as ought to be the case. Two of the rioters attempt to ride in at the tavern door, and for a while all Pandemonium seems broke loose.

To complete this picture, I must, like Asmodeus, unroof the court house, and show you a trial which I had the good fortune to witness: It was during the last war, when the vessels of Admiral Gordon were making their way up the Potomac to Alexandria, that a negro woman was arraigned for killing one of her own sex and color. She had been committed for murder, but the evidence went clearly to establish the deed to be manslaughter, inasmuch as it was done in sudden heat, and without malice aforethought. The attorney for the commonwealth waived the prosecution for murder, but quoted British authorities to show that she might be convicted of manslaughter, though committed for murder. The counsel for the accused arose, and in the most solemn manner, asked the court if it was a thing ever heard of, that an individual accused of one crime, and acquitted, should be arraigned immediately for another, under the same prosecution ? At intervals, boom—boom—boom, went the British cannon. "British authorities!" exclaimed the counsel, "British authorities, gentlemen !! Is there any one upon the bench so dead to the feelings of patriotism, as at such a moment to listen to British authorities, when the British cannon is shaking the very walls of your court house to their

foundation ?" This appeal was too cogent to be re-
sisted. Up jumped one of the justices, and protested
that it was not to be borne; let the prisoner go; away
with your British authorities! The counsel for the
accused rubbed his hands, and winked at the attorney;
the attorney stood aghast; his astonishment was too
great for utterance, and the negro was half way home
before he recovered from his amazement.

THE WAGONER.

I've often thought if I were asked
  Whose lot I envied most —
What one I thought most lightly tasked.
  Of man's unnumber'd host—
I'd say, I'd be a mountain boy,
And drive a noble team, wo, hoy!
    Wo, hoy! I'd cry,
    And lightly fly,
      Into my saddle seat;
    My rein I'd slack—
    My whip I'd crack—
      What music is so sweet?

Six blacks I'd drive, of ample chest,
  All carrying high the head,
All harness'd tight, and gayly drest
  In winkers tipp'd with red—
Oh yes, I'd be a mountain boy,
And such a team I'd drive, wo, hoy!
    Wo, hoy! I'd cry,
    The lint should fly—
      Wo, hoy! you Dobbin! Ball!
    Their feet should ring,
    And I would sing,
      I'd sing my fol de rol.

My bells would tinkle, tinkle ling,
  Beneath each bear-skin cap;
And as I saw them swing and swing,
  I'd be the merriest chap—

Yes, then I'd be a mountain boy,
And drive a jingling team, wo, hoy!
   Wo, hoy! I'd cry—
   My words should fly,
     Each horse would prick his ear;
   With tighten'd chain,
   My lumbering wain
     Would move in its career.

The golden sparks, you'd see them spring
  Beneath my horses' tread;
Each tail, I'd braid it up with string
  Of blue, or flaunting red;
So does, you know, the mountain boy,
Who drives a dashing team, wo, hoy!
   Wo, hoy! I'd cry,
   Each horse's eye
     With fire would seem to burn,
   With lifted head,
   And nostrils spread,
     They'd seem the earth to spurn.

They'd champ the bit, and fling the foam,
  As on they dragged my load;
And I would think of distant home,
  And whistle upon the road—
Oh! would I were a mountain boy—
I'd drive a six-horse team, wo, hoy!
   Wo, hoy! I'd cry—
   Now by yon sky,
     I'd sooner drive those steeds
   Than win renown,
   Or wear a crown
     Won by victorious deeds!

For crowns oft press the languid head,
  And health the wearer shuns;
And vict'ry, trampling on the dead,
  May do for Goths and Huns—
Seek them who will, they have no joys
For mountain lads, and wagon-boys.

THE SLEET.

Awake, awake, the sun is up, awake and sally forth,
We've had a rain of jewelry from out the frozen north ;
The earth is robed in dazzling white, each tree is hung
    with gems,
And diamonds, in ten thousand shapes, are hanging
    from their stems.

Each bush, and ev'ry humble shrub, with precious
    stones is strung,
And all the purest, brightest things, by handfuls round
    are flung ;
The emerald ! and the amethyst ! the topazes behold !
And here and there a ruby red is sparkling in the cold.

The chrysolite and jasper see, and that bright sardine
    stone
The holy Patmos prophet saw upon the heav'nly
    throne ;
Here all the gold of Ophir shines, with all Golconda's
    store,
And who could ever number up the countless myriads
    more ?

The Holly, in its darkest green, with crimson fruit,
    looks gay,
Enchased in solid silver too, how rich is its display !
In green and gold the shaggy Pine seems almost in a
    blaze,
With all the sun's reflected light, yet softened to the gaze.

The Cedar, ah thou favor'd tree, in Scripture it is told
They laid thee in the house of God, and covered thee
    with gold ;
But great as was king Solomon, he nor the house he
    made
Was dress'd in such magnificence as thou hast here
    display'd.

The Beech tree stands in rich array of long and shining
    threads,
Its brittle boughs all bending low to earth their droop-
    ing hea

And now and then some broken limb comes crashing
from on high,
And show'ring down a world of gems that sparkle as
they fly.

The lofty Oak! the hundred limb'd! Briareus of the
Trees!
Spreads out his pond'rous, icy arms, loud crackling in
the breeze;
And as the roused up lion "shakes the dew drops from
his mane,"
So doth the woodland monarch shake his crystals o'er
the plain.

But time would fail to tell of all that bright and starry
host
The north wind brings "to witch the world" from out
the realms of frost;
The meanest thing—the most deformed—the dry and
sapless bough,
The bramble rude—the rugged thorn, are pure and
spotless now.

"Ye councillors of earth!" come forth, "ye princes
who have gold,"
Your diadems, ye kings! bring here, the jewel'd crowns
ye hold;
Come, Woman, in thine ornaments, in all their costly
sheen,
And let them be the loveliest ones that ever graced a
queen.

This grass that's trodden under foot, this weed with
branching arms,
Thus glittering in the morning sun, hath fifty-fold their
charms;
Then cast your baubles vile away, and bend in solemn
thought
To *Him* who hath this gorgeous scene from storm and
tempest wrought.

Yet this fair pageant soon must fade before the breath
of noon,
And by the fiat from on high your wealth shall fade as
soon;

Oh! lay not worthless riches up, which "moth and rust"
    assail,
But those which at the judgment day through Christ
    will then avail.

What though the sun so soon must melt this frost-work
    and its forms,
He speaks them into life again, who rides amid the
    storms;
So, "in the twinkling of an eye," at His last trumpet
    dread,
Our bodies, fashion'd gloriously, shall rise up from the
    dead.

The sun goes up his destined way—how few do heed
    my calls!
In tears the vision melts away, "the baseless fabric"
    alls;
I too could shed some tears, alas! that this sweet scene
    is past,
For scenes as sweet it brings to mind, which fled away
    as fast.

THE SALE.

"It is the law throughout the Old Dominion,
  When some poor devil dies in peace or battle,
Th' executor must be of the opinion
  His goods are perishing, and sell each chattel;
Whatever treads on hoof or flies on pinion—
  Hogs, horses, cows, and every sort of cattle—
Cups, saucers, swingle-trees and looking glasses—
Ploughs, pots and pans, tea-kettles and jackasses."

A man who never quotes, it has been said, will in
return never be quoted. By way, therefore, of quoting,
and at the same time of being quoted, I have quoted a
poem of my own, which "will never be published,"
written in attempted imitation of Beppo, and describing
a sale in Virginia. Who has not seen something like
the following staring him in the face, on the side of a
store or tavern, or upon the post of a sign-board where
several roads meet? "I shel purceed to sell to the

highest bidder, on Saterday the 3d of Janewary next, at Blank, all the housol and kitchen ferniter of the late David Double, Esq. together with all the horses, muels, sheep and hoges. Cash on all sums of five dollars and under, and a credit of twelve mont, on the ballance. Bond with aproved sekurity will be required," &c. Such a notification as the above, which is copied verbatim et spellatim, operates like an electric shock on a whole neighborhood in that portion of the country in which I reside, especially upon that part of the population which can least afford to buy bargains. The temptation of long credit is too great to be resisted, although no calculations of the ultimate ability to pay are ever made. The grand desideratum is to obtain the necessary security, and to purchase to a greater amount than five dollars. I am myself infected by this prevailing malady, and frequently buy what is of no manner of use to me, simply because no cash is required, and bonds are hard to collect, and suits may be put off by continuances; and matters of this sort, after all, may be settled by executors and administrators. Among the rest, therefore, on the day appointed by the aforesaid notification, I mounted my horse, and sallied out upon the road leading to Blank, and fell in with a large party going to the sale, principally managers, as they call themselves now-a-days, on the neighboring estates. Formerly they were yclept overseers, but the term is falling into disuse, as conveying the idea of something derogatory. They were mounted in every variety of style; there were long tails, and bob tails, and nicked tails; and I saw at least one sheep skin saddle and grapevine bridle.

By-the-by, talking of grapevines, what a country ours is for this invaluable article. Here is no need of hemp manufactories. Nature, in her exuberant goodness, has supplied an abundance of primitive rope, which is just as convenient and efficacious as the best cordage, whether a man wants to hang himself or a dog—whether he wants a cap for his fence, a backband for his plough-horse, a pair of leading lines, or a girth for his saddle. Why should we be the advocates of a tariff, when nature supplies us in peace or war with this and many other articles of the first necessity, among which I once heard a Chotanker enumerate mint. "Why," said he, "should we fear a dissolution of the union, a separation of the north from the south, when there is not a sprig of mint in all New England?" When this was said, peradventure it might be true; but, to my certain knowledge, at this day the word julap is well understood much farther north than Mason's and Dixon's line. Pardon me, reader, this digression—for I am mounted to-day on a rough-going, headstrong animal, that will have his own way, and wants to turn aside into every by-path which he sees, and is as "*willyard a powny*" as that ridden by Dumbiedikes, when he followed Jeanie Deans to lend her the purse of gold.

But to return.—I cannot let this opportunity slip of singling out one of this group of horsemen for description, that you may have a graphic sketch of the sort of folks and horses that live hereabouts. Wert thou ever upon Hoecake Ridge? and hast thou ever met in winter a thorough-bred native of that region, mounted upon his little shaggy pony, "skelping on through dub and mire," like Tam O'Shanter? Here he was to-day, in his element, dressed in nankin pantaloons and a thin cotton jacket, and riding in the teeth of a strong northwester, singing "Life let us cherish." His saddle had no skirts, having been robbed of those useless appendages by some rogue who wanted a pair of brogues; his bridle had as many knots as the sea serpent. But my business is not so much with him as with his pony, whose head and neck may be aptly represented by a maul and its handle. His tail is six inches long, and standing at an angle of forty-five degrees with his back; his hair is long and shaggy; he is cat-hammed, and his chest so narrow that his forelegs almost touch one another; his eyes snap fire when you plague him. You may talk of improving the breed of horses. Tell me not of your Eclipses, your Henrys—of Arabians or Turks. They may be all very well in their places, but this pony is the animal for my country. He can bite the grass which is absolutely invisible to human eyes, and subsist upon it. If you would give him six ears of corn twice a-day, he would be almost too fat to travel. He never stumbles. Give him the rein, and he will pick his path as carefully as a lady. His powers of endurance exceed the camel's. His master is a sot, and his horse will stand all night at a tippling shop, gnawing a fence rail; he almost prefers it to a corn-stalk which has been lying out all winter, his common food. When his master comes forth and mounts, he studies attitudes. If the rider reel to the right, the pony leans to the starboard side; if to the left, he tacks to suit him. If the master fall, he falls clear, having no girth to his saddle, and the pony does not waste time in useless meditation upon accidents that will happen to the best of us, but moves homeward with accelerated velocity, leaping every obstacle in his way to his brush stable.

It was my good fortune to drop in alongside of the man who was mounted upon this incomparable animal, and complimenting him upon his philosophy in the selection of his song, and on the dexterity of his horse, I soon found he was a great politician, and we chatted most agreeably until our arrival at the place of sale. He was a violent ——, but not a word of politics; literature and politics are different matters altogether. You may be a great politician, you know, without a particle of literature. Politicians are the last people in the world to bear a joke; and if I were even to glance at the discourse of my neighbors, there are many who would not submit to this interference with their exclusive business; they would see in it "more devils than vast hell can hold." The world must therefore be content to lose the humor of my singular acquaintance, as I cannot possibly do justice to his conceptions without the mention of names. I shall die, though, unless I find some occasion of disclosing them, for old Hardcastle's man Diggory was never more diverted at his story of the grouse in the gun-room, than I was at the political conceits of my Hoecake-ridger.

Having arrived at Blank, we *hung* our horses, as

Virginians always do after riding them, and entered the grounds before a venerable looking building which had been completely embowelled, and its contents were piled in promiscuous heaps in various parts of the yard. Within the great house, as it is usually styled, was already assembled, around a blazing fire, a crowd of exceedingly noisy folks, all talking at once, and nobody apparently listening. The names of our leading men sounded on every side, and the Tower of Babel never witnessed a greater confusion of tongues. For my own part, it always makes me melancholy to contemplate this inroad of Goths and Vandals upon apartments which were once perhaps so sacred, and kept in order with such sedulous attention. It seems a profanation— a want of respect for the recently dead, and a cruel outrage upon the feelings of the surviving family. Nothing escapes the prying eye of curiosity—the rude footstep invades the very penetralia. The household gods, the *dii penates*, are all upturned; and mirth and jesting reign amidst the precincts of woe. I felt like a jackall tearing open the grave for my prey. The crier, the high priest of these infernal orgies, now came forward with his badge of office, the jug of whiskey, and announced that the sale would commence as soon as he could wet his whistle, which he proceeded to do, and then began to ply his customers. It is wonderful to think how much ingenuity has been displayed in finding out metaphors to describe the detestable act of tippling. The renowned biographer of Washington and Marion has embodied a number of these in one of his minor performances; but several which I heard to-day were new to me, and escaped his researches; thus I heard one upbraid another for being too fond of "tossing his head back," while a third invited his companion to "rattle the stopper,"—and upon my taking a very moderate drink, and so weak that a temperance man would scarcely have frowned upon me, I was clapped on the shoulder, and jeered for my fondness for the creature, since I was willing to swallow an ocean of water to get at a drop. In a very short time

3

the liquid fire of the Greeks ran through the veins of the crowd, and they were quickly ripe for bidding.

"Inspiring bold John Barleycorn,
What dangers thou canst make us scorn ;
Wi' tippenny we fear no evil—
Wi' usquebaugh we'll face the devil."

The "swats sae reamed" in their noddles, that every thing sold at a price far beyond its value, and our crier became so exceedingly facetious, and cracked so many excellent ironical jokes, that it is a pity they should be lost. Being unskilled, however, in stenography, I could not take down his words, and only remember that every untrimmed old field colt was a regular descendant of Eclipse ; the long nosed hogs were uuquestionably Parkinson ; the sheep Merinoes ; the cattle, which were notoriously all horn, were short horns, &c. &c. They seemed to me to be a scurvy set of animals ; but those who saw them through a *glass darkly,* seemed to entertain a very different opinion. The "mirth and fun grew fast and furious," "till first a caper sin anither" "they lost their reasons a' thegither," and the sale closed in one wild, uproarious scuffle for every thing at any price whatever.

It now became necessary to return home, an important consideration which had been wholly overlooked ; and the difficulty of mounting our horses having been overcome after many trials, we began to "witch the world with feats of noble horsemanship." Such "racing and chasing" had not been seen since the days of Cannobie lea, and quizzing became the order of the evening. Perceiving the mettlesome nature of my steed, my friend, the politician and philosopher, seemed resolved upon unhorsing me, notwithstanding my entreaties that he would forbear, and by dint of riding violently up to me, and shouting out at the top of his voice, he so alarmed my nag, that he seized the bit between his teeth, and away I flew, John Gilpin like, to the infinite amusement of my persecutor, until I was safely deposited in a mud hold, near my own gate, from whence I had to finish my journey on foot, and appear before my helpmate in a condition that reflected greatly upon my character. As a finale to this mortifying business, my purchases were brought home the next day, and were most unceremoniously thrown out of doors by my wife, as utterly useless, being literally sans eyes, sans teeth, sans every thing; cracked pitchers, broken pots, spiders without legs, jugs without handles, *et id genus omne.*

THE MOCKINGBIRD.

Come, listen! oh list! to that soft dying strain
Of my Mockingbird, up on the house-top again;
He comes every night to these old ruined walls,
Where soft as the moonlight his melody falls.
Oh! what can the bulbub or nightingale chant,
In the climes which they love, and the groves which
       they haunt,
More thrilling and wild than the song I have heard,
In the stillness of night, from my sweet Mockingbird!

I saw him to-day, on his favorite tree,
Where he constantly comes in his glory and glee,
Perch'd high on a limb, which was standing out far
Above all the rest, like a tall taper spar:
The wind, it was wafting that limb to and fro,
And he rode up and down, like a skiff in a blow,
When it sinks with the billow, and mounts with its
       swell;
He knew I was watching—he knew it full well.

He folded his pinions and swelled out his throat,
And mimick'd each bird in its own native note,—
The Thrush and the Robin, the Redbird and all—
And the Partridge would whistle and answer his call;
Then stopping his carol, he seemed to prepare,
By the flirt of his wings, for a flight in the air,
When rising sheer upward, he wheeled down again,
And took up his song where he left off the strain.

Would you cage such a creature, and draggle his plumes?
Condemn him to prison, the worst of all dooms?

Take from him the pleasure of flying so free ?
And deny him his ride on the wind wafted-tree ?
Would you force him to droop within merciless bars,
When earth is all sunshine, or heaven all stars ?
Forbid it, oh mercy ! and grant him the boon
Of a sail in the sun and a song to the moon.

What a gift he possesses of throat and of lungs !
The gift apostolic—the gift of all tongues !
Ah ! could he but utter the lessons of love,
To wean us from earth and to waft us above,
What siren could tempt us to wander again ?
We'd seek but the siren outpouring that strain—
Would listen to nought but his soft dying fall,
As he sat all alone on some old ruined wall.

[For the Southern Literary Messenger.]

INTERESTING RUINS ON THE RAPPAHANNOCK.

MR. EDITOR.—As I find you are about to establish
a sort of Literary Emporium, to which every man, no
matter how trifling his capital of ideas, may send his
productions, I have resolved to transmit to you, my
small wares and merchandize. The relation I shall
bear to your other correspondents, will be that which
the vender of trifles in a town bears to the wealthy
merchant; and, therefore, I shall assume an appropri-
ate title, and under this humble signature, shall con-
sider myself at liberty to offer you any thing I may
have, without order or method, and just as I can lay
my hands upon it. My head is somewhat like Domi-
nie Sampson's, which, as well as I remember, re-
sembled a pawnbroker's shop, where a goodly store of
things were piled together, but in such confusion, he
could never find what he wanted. When I get hold of
any thing, however, I will send it to you, and if it be
worth nothing, why, just "martyr it by a pipe."

"Here lived, so might it seem to fancy's eye,
The lordly Barons of our feudal day ;
On every side, lo ! grandeur's relics lie
Scattered in ruin o'er their coffin'd clay.—

How vain for man, short sighted man, to say
  What course the tide of human things shall take !
How little dreamed the Founder, that decay,
  So soon his splendid edifice should shake,
  And of its high pretence, a cruel mock'ry make."

There cannot be a more striking exemplification of the powerful influence of laws upon the state of society, than is exhibited on the banks of the rivers in the lower part of Virginia. How many spacious structures are seen there, hastening to decay, which were once the seats of grandeur and a magnificent hospitality! The barons of old were scarcely more despotic over their immediate demesnes, than were the proprietors of these noble mansions, with their long train of servants and dependents; their dicta were almost paramount to law, throughout their extensive and princely possessions. But since the introduction of republican institutions, and the alteration in the laws respecting the descent of property, and more especially since the "docking of entails," a total change has been effected. Our castles are crumbling on every side— estates are subdivided into minuter portions, instead of being transmitted to the eldest son ; and so complete is the revolution in sentiment, that he would be deemed a savage, who would now leave the greater part of his family destitute, for the sake of aggrandizing an individual. It is not unusual to find a son in possession of the once splendid establishment of his fathers, with scarcely paternal acres enough to afford him sustenance, and hardly wood enough to warm a single chamber of all his long suite of apartments. The old family coach, with his mother and sisters, lumbers along after a pair of superannuated skeletons, and some faithful domestic, like Caleb Balderstone, is put to the most desperate shifts to support the phantom of former grandeur. Debts are fast swallowing up the miserable remnant of what was once a principality, while some wealthy democrat of the neighborhood, who has accumulated large sums by despising an empty show, "is ready to foreclose his mortgage, and send the wretched heir of Ravenswood to mingle with the

3*

Bucklaws and Craigengelts of the west. Many a
story of deep interest might be written upon the old
state of things in Virginia, if we possessed some inde-
fatigable Jedediah Cleishbotham, to collect the tradi-
tions of our ancestors.

Those who took part in our revolutionary struggle,
were too much enlightened not to foresee these conse-
quences, and therefore deserve immortal credit for their
disinterested opposition to Great Britain. Had they
been aristocrats instead of the purest republicans, they
would surely have thrown their weight into the oppo-
site scale. We do not estimate enough the merit of
the rich men of that day. The danger is now past—
the mighty guerdon won—the storm is gone over, and
the sun beams brightly : but though bright our day, it
was then a dark unknown—dark as the hidden path
beyond the grave—and it was nobly dared to risk their
all in defence of liberty. They knew that freedom
spurned a vain parade, and would not bow in homage
to high-born wealth; yet their splendid possessions
were staked upon the desperate throw, and the glorious
prize was won. Such were not the anticipations of the
founders of these establishments ; but such was surely
the merit of their sons ; and it is painful to think how
few, of all who engaged in that noble struggle, have
been handed down to fame. Many a one, whose name
has been loudly sounded through the earth, would
have shrunk from such a sacrifice, and clung to his
paternal hearth ; and yet these modern Curtii, who re-
nounced the advantages of birth, and leaped into the
gulf for their country's sake, have not won a single
garland for their Roman worth.

There is a scene in the county of Lancaster, where
these reflections pressed themselves very forcibly upon
my mind. Imagine an ample estate on the margin of
the Rappahannock, with its dilapidated mansion house,
the ruins of an extensive wall, made to arrest the in-
roads of the waves, as if the proprietor felt himself a
Canute, and able to stay the progress of the sea—a
church of the olden times, beautiful in structure, and
built of brick brought from England, then the home of

our people. Like Old Mortality, I love to chisel out the moss covered letters of a tombstone; and below I send you the result of my labors, with a request that some of your correspondents will take the trouble to give you a faithful translation of the Latin inscription. The only difficulty consists in the want of knowledge of the names of the officers under the colonial government. The epitaph will show by whom the church was built, and the motive for its erection. In the yard are three tombstones, conspicuous above all the rest, beneath which repose the bones of the once lordly proprietor of the soil, and his two wives. How vain are human efforts, to perpetuate by monuments, the memory of the great! The sepulchre of Osymandus is said by Diodorus, to have been a mile and a quarter in circumference. It had this inscription: "I am Osymandus, king of kings. If any one is desirous to know how great I am and where I lie, let him surpass any of my works." With more propriety might he have said, let him search out my works; for we are left to conjecture the very site of his tomb. It would be easy to extend this narrative, but perhaps what struck me as interesting would be unworthy a place in your Literary Messenger.

The Epitaph.

H. S. E.

Vir honorabilis Robertus Carter, Armiger, qui genus honestum dotibus eximiis, moribus antiquis illustravit. Collegium Gulielmi et Mariæ temporibus difficilimis propugnavit.

GUBERNATOR.

Senatus Rogator et Quæster, sub serenissimis Principibus Gulielmo, Anna, Georgio 1 mo et 2 do.

Translation.

HERE LIES

Robert Carter, esq., an honorable man, who exalted his high birth by noble endowments and pure morals. He sustained the College of William and Mary in the most trying times.

HE WAS GOVERNOR,

Speaker of the House, and Treasurer, under the most serene Princess William, Anne, George the 1st and 2d.

A publicis consiliis consilii per sexennium præses, plus annum Coloniæ Præfectus cum regiam dignitatem tam publicum libertatem æquali jure asseruit. Opibus amphissimis bene partis instructus, ædem hanc sacram In Deum pietatis grande monumentum, propriis sumptibus extruxit.

LOCUPLETAVIT.

In omnes quos humiter incepit, nec pareus hospes. Liberalilatem insignem testantur debita munifice remissa.

Primo Juditham, Johannis Armistead Armigeri filiam, deinde Betty, generosa Landonorum stirpe oriundam sibi connubio junctas habuit. E quibus prolem numerosam suscepit.

In qua erudienda pecuniæ vim maximam insumpsit.

Tandem honorum et dierum satur cum omnia vitæ munera egregiæ præstitisset obiit Pri. Non. Aug. An. Dom. 1732, Æt. 69.

Miseri solamen, viduæ præsidium, orbi patrem, ademptum lugent.

Elected Speaker by the Public Assembly, for six years, and Governor for more than a year, he equally upheld the regal dignity and public freedom.

Possessed of ample wealth, honourably acquired, he built and endowed, at his own expense, this sacred edifice, a lasting monument of his piety to God.

Entertaining his friends with kindness, he was neither a prodigal nor a thrifty host.

His first wife was Judith, daughter of John Armistead, esq.; his second, Betty, a descendant of the noble family of the Landons, by whom he had many children, on whose education he expended a considerable portion of his property.

At length, full of honors and years, having discharged all the duties of an exemplary life, he departed from this world on the 4th day of August, 1732, in the 69th year of his age.

The wretched, the widowed and the orphans, bereaved of their comfort, protector and father, alike lament his loss.

THE GREAT WESTERN.

She comes, she comes, the ship,
  The lion flag flies o'er,
Fresh from her ocean trip,
  Roar for her, cannon—roar!
A vast and moving mass of black,
  The mighty Western! hail!
She's ploughing up her foaming track
  As ploughs the sea the whale.

In harbor now she rides,
  The earth and ocean ring,
Ten thousands throng her sides
  Welcoming—welcoming—
Triumphal entry into Rome,
  The triumph Rome decreed
To grace her victor's coming home,
  This triumph shall exceed.

Rome's was but empty show
  Of kings as captives led,
Wealth rifled from her foe
  Whose blood too oft was shed;
No triumph this for conquest, yes,
  A conquest great, 'tis mind's,
'Tis human skill we throng to bless
  For vict'ry o'er the winds.

It was not on white wings,
  That through the seas she drave
This palace fit for kings,
  This world upon the wave;
A giant vast she holds in chains
  Down in her donjon keep,
To break his fetters there he strains,
  And drives her o'er the deep.

A Cyclop at his forge,
  He shakes her thick ribb'd frame,
E'en hell could not disgorge
  More dark and lurid flame;

He leaps and pitches with a groan,
　His breath's a cloud of smoke,
But all in vain, that hollow moan
　Hath o'er Atlantic broke.

Oh God! and what is man?
　What bounds his daring soul?
His all of life a span—
　Would he thy seas control?
His ships by mighty winds careen'd,
　Their timbers all uptorn,
He conjures up this fearful fiend,
　And laughs the winds to scorn.

And was it not full bold
　To dare the raging sea?
But he must cage and hold
　This monster, which, if free,
Would in a moment bathe in gore
　Each man who treads that deck,
And drown the tempest with his roar,
　And make that ship a wreck.

A health to Bristol's sons!
　Whose ship hath won the goal,
Her ship of thousand tons,
　And mine of hidden coal;
"Her march is on the mountain wave,
　Her home is on the deep,"
A shout for her gigantic slave
　Down in her donjon keep.

A wreath for Fulton! Watt!!
　One for the glorious dead,
Oh! be it not forgot
　A wreath for genius fled;
One blended wreath for those great minds
　Who bodied forth that ship,
Careering thus mid waves and winds
　Upon the pathless deep.

God speed thee, Kraken ship!
　Back to old England's shores,
And many a golden trip
　Across the main be yours;

The Lion and the Eagle shall
Have done with senseless wrath,
And each shall move majestical
Upon his chosen path.

THE MECHANICIAN AND UNCLE SIMON.

About the period of what *"I am gaun to tell,"* the
ancient aristocracy of Virginia had passed through its
death struggle; the times when the rich were every
thing, and the poor nothing, had passed away; and the
high pretensions of the sons of the Cavaliers had yield-
ed to the more levelling opinions of the Roundheads.
The badges of distinction, such as coats of arms and
liveries, had become too odious to be generally kept up;
occasionally the latter were seen, but so rarely that
they looked like the spectres of departed greatness, and
excited a feeling of contempt or pity for the weakness
of the master, rather than respect for his wealth and
rank. There was once a class of people, nevertheless,
who retained all their attachment to these distinctive
marks; and indeed they do so to this day: I mean the
class of servants who belonged to the old families.
They were the veriest aristocrats upon earth, and hated
with the most unrelenting hatred, all the ignoble blood
of the land, and deeply deplored the transition of pro-
perty from the nobles to the serfs. Though their own
"ancient but ignoble blood" had literally almost *"crept
through scoundrels ever since the flood,"* they detested
the poor and adored the rich.

I shall never forget the fall of the year ——. I had
just graduated at one of our northern colleges, and re-
ceived my two diplomas, with their red ribbons and
seals attached. They were deposited by my good
friend, Andrew McMackin, the most expert diploma
rigger in all the village, in a plain cylindrical paste-
board, for safe keeping, and would have remained there
probably to this day, unmolested, had not the rats made
an inroad upon them, and in a single night demolished
sigillum and signature—all that it had cost me years of

hard labor to obtain—aye, and twenty dollars to boot.
Not satisfied, I suppose, with the attestation of the
president and venerable board of trustees, they were
desirous of adding their own *ratification* to my preten-
sions to science. Be that as it may, full of delightful
anticipation at the prospect of returning to my native
state, after an absence of four years, I took my seat in
the mail stage, and travelled three hundred miles with-
out going to bed. ·Such a journey at this day of steam-
boat and railroad car, would be nothing, but at that time
it was a great undertaking, and attended with much fa-
tigue. The vehicles were crazy, and often broke
down, and the passengers had the pleasure of paying
dearly for the privilege of walking many a mile through
the mud.

At length I arrived at the little town of F——, the
end of my journey on the great mail route, where I ex-
pected to meet with some kind of conveyance to take me
into the country to my uncle's. As I leaped from the
carriage to the pavement, where many loiterers were
gathered to witness the arrival of the stage, I found
myself suddenly locked in the arms of some one who
exclaimed, "*There he is, the very moral of his grand-
papa!* God bless your honor, how do ye do? I'm so
glad to see you." Extricating myself with some de-
gree of embarrassment, because of the crowd around
me, I perceived that the salutation proceeded from one
of our old servants, who stood gazing upon me with
the most benevolent smile. His appearance was quite
outré to one who had lived so long at the north. His
old and faded livery was blue, turned up with yellow;
he held in his hand a horseman's cap, without the
bear-skin; his boots had once been white-topped, but
could no longer claim that distinctive epithet; like
Sir Hudibras, he wore but one spur, though probably
for a different reason; his high forehead glistened in
the sun, and his slightly grey hair was combed neatly
back, and queued behind with an eelskin so tight that
he could hardly wink his eyes, exhibiting a face re-
markably intelligent and strongly marked, with a nose
uncommonly high and hawkbilled for a negro. Per-

ceiving my embarrassment. he drew back with a very courtly bow, declaring he was so glad to see me, he had forgotten himself and made too free. I made haste to assure him that he had not—gave him a hearty shake by the hand—called him Uncle Simon, a name he had always been accustomed to from me, and drawing him aside, overwhelmed him with questions about every body and every thing at home. "Tell me," said I, "how is my uncle?" "I thank you, sir, quite hearty, and much after the old sort—full of his projjecks, heh! heh! perpechil motion, and what not." "What," said I, "is he at that still?" "Oh yes—oh yes—and carridges to go without horses; God love you, Mass Ned, I don't think they can go without animel nater." "And how does my aunt like all this?" "Ah!" said he, putting up his hands with an air of disgust, "she can't abide it—things go on badly. You 'member my four greys? so beautiful!—my four in hand!—all gone, all sold. Why, sir, I could whistle them hawses to the charrut jest as easy as snap my finger. Our fine London charrut, too! that's gone, and my poor Missis, your aunt, has nothin to ride in but a nasty pitiful park phæton." "I am sorry to hear it, Simon." "Why, Mass Ned, what mek you all let dem *Demmy Cats* sarve you so? What you call 'em? Publicans? yes, I'd cane 'em as old master used to do." "But Simon, how is Cousin Mary?" "Miss Mary? oh, Miss Mary is a beauty; gay as a young filly, and she walks upon her pasterns."

"Well, well," said I, interrupting him, "Simon let us be off; what have you brought for me to ride?" "Old Reglus, sir, your old favorite." Having taken some refreshment, and transferred my clothes to the portmanteau, I mounted Regulus, who still showed his keeping. He was a bright bay, and his hair was as glossy as silk, under Simon's management; his eye still glanced its fire, and his wide nostrils gave token of his wind. He knew me, I shall ever believe it, for my voice made him prick his ears, as if listening to the music of former days. It seemed to inspire him with new life; he flew like an arrow, and Simon found it

4

impossible to keep up with me, mounted as he was on a high trotting, raw boned devil, that made the old man bound like a trap ball, whenever he missed his up-and-down-postilion movement. His figure, thus bobbing in front of a monstrous portmanteau and bearskin, was so ludicrous I could not forbear laughing; and reining up my steed, I told him I would ride slower, for the sake of conversation with him. "Do, my good sir," cried he, "for this vile garran will knock the breath out of my body. If I had but my old hawse, Grey Dick, alive agin—that hawse, Mass Ned, was the greatest hawse upon the face of the yearth; I rod him ninety miles the hottest day that ever came from heaven; when I got through our outer gate, he seized the bit between his teeth, and run away with me, and never stopped till he got clean into the stable. Whenever I fed him, I was 'bliged to shet the stable door and go away, for if he heard me move, or a stirrup jingle, he wouldn't eat another mouthful, but stood with his head up, and his eyes flying about, impatient for me to mount."

I knew this was a moment to put in a leading question to bring out a story I had heard a thousand times. "That was not the horse that ran away with you when a boy?" "No—no—that was Whalebone; your grandpapa used always to go to court in his coach and six; I can see him now, in his great big wig, hanging down upon his shoulders, and powdered as white as a sheet. I was then a little shaver, and always went behind the carriage to open the gates. Waitinman George rod the old gentleman's ridin hawse Bearskin, and led Mass Bobby's hawse Whalebone; Mass Bobby rod in the carriage with old master. Well, one day, what should George do but put me up upon Whalebone, as big a devil as ever was; soonever I got upon him, off he went by the coach as hard as he could stave; old master hallooed and bawled—he'll kill him—he'll kill him—George, how dare you put Simon upon Whalebone? Pshey! the more he hallooed the more Whalebone run. I pulled and pulled until I got out of sight, and turned down the quarter stretch, and then *I did*

give him the timber—Flying Childers was nothing to
him. When old master got home, there I was, with
Whalebone as cool as a *curcumber*. I made sure I
should get a caning, but all he said was 'D—n the
fellow! I blieve he could ride old Whalebone's tail
off'—heh! heh! heh!" I am sorry I cannot do more
justice to the eloquence of Simon, who excelled in all
the arts of oratory. His eyes spoke as much as his
tongue; his gestures were vehement, but quite appro-
priate; he uttered some words in as startling a voice
as Henry Clay, and his forefinger did as much execu-
tion as John Randolph's. As to his political opinions,
he was the most confirmed aristocrat, and thought it the
birthright of his master's family to ride over the poor,
booted and spurred. It was his delight to tell of his
meeting one day, as he swept along the road with his
smoking four in hand, a poor man on horseback, whom
he contemptuously styled a *Johnny*. He ordered the
man to give the road; but as he did not obey him as
readily as he desired, he resolved to punish him. By a
dexterous wheel of his leaders, he brought the chariot
wheel in contact with the fellow's knee, and shaved
every button off as nicely as he could have shaved his
beard with a razor.

But enough of Simon. I beguiled the way by draw-
ing him out upon his favorite topics, until we got within
sight of my uncle's house, a fine old mansion, with an
avenue of cedars a mile in length. They had been
kept for several generations neatly trimmed, and he
who had dared to mar their beauty with an axe, would
have been considered a felon, and met his fate without
benefit of clergy. I have lived to see them all cut down
by the ruthless hand of an overseer, who sees no beauty
in any thing but a cornstalk. However, this is wan-
dering from my present theme. Then they were in all
their evergreen loveliness, and I hailed them as my
ancient friends, as I galloped by them, with a joyous
feeling at approaching the scene of my childhood. The
folding doors soon flew wide open, and the whole
family rushed out to meet me, with true-hearted, old
fashioned Virginia promptitude. I must not attempt

to describe a meeting which is always better imagined than described. Let it suffice, that after the most affectionate greeting, which extended to every servant about the premises, I was ushered to my bed room at a late hour, with as much of state as could be mustered about the now decaying establishment, and soon sunk into a profound slumber, well earned by the toils and fatigues of my journey. Early the next morning, before I left my room, my excellent and revered uncle paid me a visit, and ordered in the never failing julap,—*such a one as would have done honor to Chotank.* At the same time he suggested to me that he would greatly prefer my taking a mixture of his own, which he extolled as much as Don Quixote did his balsam to Sancho, or Dr. Sangrado his warm water to Gil Blas. It was a pleasant beverage, he said, compounded of an acid and an alkali. He had discovered, by close observation, that all diseases had their origin in acid, and that alkali of course was the grand panacea; even poisons were acids, and he had no doubt that he should be able to form a concrete mass, by means of beef gall and alkali, -which would resemble and equal in virtue the *mad stone.* If I felt the slightest acidity of stomach, I would find myself relieved by one of his powders. He had written to Dr. Rush on the subject, and he showed me a letter from that gentleman, at which he laughed heartily, and in which the doctor protested he might as well attempt to batter the rock of Gibraltar with mustard seed shot, as to attack the yellow fever with alkali. I could not help smiling at the earnestness of my dear uncle, and assured him that I had no doubt of the virtues of his medicine, but as I was quite well, I would rather try the anti-fogmatic; and if I should feel indisposed I would resort to his panacea; although I secretly resolved to have as little to do with it as Gil Blas had with water.

Having dressed myself, and descended to the breakfast room, I there met my aunt and cousin, who soon made me acquainted with the present condition of the family. Every thing was fast declining, in consequence of the total absorption of the mind of my uncle in his visionary schemes; and I saw abundant evidence of the wreck of his fortune, in the absence of a thousand comforts and elegancies which I had been accustomed to behold. He soon joined us, and such was his excellence of character, that we carefully avoided casting the smallest damp upon his ardor. Indeed, he was a man of great natural talent, and much acquired information, and was far above the ridicule which was sometimes played off upon him by his more ignorant neighbors. I almost begin to think that *we* were the mistaken ones, when I look around and see the perfection of many of his schemes, which I then thought wholly impracticable. When old Simon thought that a carriage could never go without *animel nater* he certainly never dreamed of a rail road car, nor of the steam carriages of England; and when my uncle gravely told me that he should fill up his ice house, and manufacture ice as he wanted it in summer, by letting out air highly condensed in a tight copper vessel upon water, I did not dream of the execution of the plan by some French projector. I must not be thus diffuse, or I shall weary the patience of my reader.

A ride was proposed after breakfast, and my uncle immediately invited me to try his newly invented vehicle, which could not be overset. "I have constructed," said he, "a carriage with a moveable perch, by means of which the body swings out horizontally, whenever the wheels on one side pass over any high obstacle or ground more elevated than the other wheels rest upon; and I shall be glad to exhibit it to a young man who is fresh from college, and must be acquainted with the principles of mechanics. I readily accepted his proposal, although I trembled for my neck, but declared I had no mechanical turn whatever, and could not construct a wheelbarrow. He was sorry to hear this, as he was in hopes I would be the depository of all his schemes, and bring them to perfection, in case of his death, for the benefit of his family. We soon set off on our ride, and Simon was the driver. As I anticipated, in descending a hill where the ground presented great inequality, the whole party were capsized, and nothing saved our

4*

bones but the lowness of our vehicle. Never shall I forget the chagrin of my uncle, nor the impatient contemptuous look of Simon, as he righted the carriage; he did not dare to expostulate with his master, but could not forbear saying that he had never met with such an accident when he drove his four greys. "Ah, there is the cause," said my uncle, much gratified at having an excuse for his failure, "Simon is evidently intoxicated; old man, never presume to drive me again when you are not perfectly sober; you will ruin the most incomparable contrivance upon earth." Simon contented himself with a sly wink at me, and we made the best of our way home; my uncle promising me another trial in a short time, and I determining to avoid it, if human ingenuity could contrive the means.

The next day, as I was amusing myself with a book, my uncle came in from his work-shop, with a face beaming with pleasure; and entering the room, proceeded in the most careful manner to close all the doors; and producing a small crooked stick, said to me with a mysterious air, "My boy, this stick, as small and inconsiderable as it seems to be, has made your fortune. It is worth a million of dollars, for it has suggested to me an improvement in my machine for producing perpetual motion, which puts the thing beyond all doubt." "Is it possible," cried I, "that so small a stick can be worth so much?" "Yes, depend upon it—and I carefully closed the doors, because I would not be overheard for the world. Some fellow might slip before me to the patent office, and rob me of my treasure." I observed that nobody was there who could possibly do so. "Yes, somebody might be casually passing, and I cannot be too vigilant. I take it for granted," he resumed, "that you are apprised of the grand desideratum in this business. You do not imagine, with the ignorant, that I expect to make matter last longer than God intended; the object is to get a machine to keep time so accurately, that it may be used at sea, to ascertain the longitude with precision. Do you know that a gentleman has already constructed a time piece, for which the Board of Longitude paid him fifty thousand pounds; but owing to the metallic expansion it would not be entirely accurate." I answered that I had not so much as heard of the Board of Longitude—and he proceeded to explain his improvement, of which I did not comprehend a syllable. All that I felt sure of, although I did not tell him so, was that he would not succeed in realizing the million of dollars; and accordingly, when admitted, as a great favor into his sanctum sanctorum, the work-shop, to witness his machine put in motion, it stood most perversely still after one revolution, and "*some slight alteration,*" remained to be made to the end of the chapter,—until hope became extinct in every breast, save that of the projector.

I could fill a volume with anecdotes of this sort, but I will add only one, as descriptive of the very great height to which visionary notions may be carried. My uncle was a federalist, and of course hated Buonaparte from the bottom of his soul. He told me, as a profound secret, that he had discovered the means of making an old man young again, by removing from him the atmospheric pressure, and that nothing deterred him from making the discovery, but the fear that Buonaparte would attach his machinery to a body of soldiers, and fly across the British Channel, and thus light down in the midst of England, and make an easy conquest of the only barrier left upon earth to secure the liberties of mankind. *Eheu! jam satis!* thought I.

In this way did my poor uncle spend his time, to the utter ruin of a fine estate, which was surrendered to the management of that most pestilent of the human race, an overseer,—who would not at last be at the trouble of furnishing the old gentleman with wood enough to keep him warm in his spacious edifice. The means he resorted to, to reprove the overseer, were not less characteristic and laughable than many of his singular notions. One very cold day he sent for him; the man attended, and was ushered with much solemnity into an apartment where a single chump was burning feebly in the chimney place, and a table was standing in the centre of the room, covered with papers, pen and ink. My uncle received him with unusual courtesy, and ordered the servant to set a chair for Mr. Corncob by the *fire*, with a peculiar emphasis on the word. "I have sent for you, Mr. Corncob," said he, "to get you to witness my will.. You see, sir," pointing at the same time to the fire, "you see, sir, how small a probability there is that I shall survive the present winter. I am anxious to settle my affairs previous to my being attacked by the pleurisy, and have therefore sent for you to aid me in doing so." This was a severe reproof, and the man having done as he was bid, retired with an air the most sheepish imaginable.

I fill up the picture, by stating that I married my cousin, and inherited the estate in due course of time; but a mortgage swallowed it up as effectually as an earthquake—and poor old Simon died of a broken heart, when Regulus was knocked off at the sale of his master's property, at twenty dollars, to the man whom he hated of all others, Christopher Corncob, Esquire.

THE HEART.

Man's heart! what melancholy things
　　Are garnered up in thee!—
What solace unto life it brings
　　That none the heart can see—
'Tis shut from every human eye,
　　Close curtain'd from the view;
The scene alike of grief and joy—
　　Man's hell and heaven too.

Should all mankind combine to tear
　　The curtain, thrown around,
Their labor would be spent in air—
　　It is his hallowed ground:
Within thy magic circle, Heart!
　　So potent is his spell,
No human hand hath strength to part
　　Or turn aside the veil.

In sadness there's a pleasure soft,
  "Which mourners only know;"
My heart affords this treasure oft,
  And there I love to go;
It is the chosen spot where I
  Can live my life anew—
My Home!—my Castle!—my Serai!
  Which none must dare break through.

In thee, my Heart! I am alone
  Quite unrestrain'd and free,
Thou'rt hung with pictures all my own,
  And drawn for none but me;
All that in secret passes there,
  Forever I can hide;
Ambition—love—or dark despair—
  My jealousy—or pride.

Yes, when ambitious—ardent—young—
  I thought the world my own,
My glowing portraits there were hung;
  How have their colors flown!—
Some are by time defaced so far
  I look on them with pain;
But time nor nothing else can mar
  The portrait of my Jane.

I placed her there who won my soul;
  No creature saw the maid;
I gazed in bliss, without control,
  On every charm displayed:
It was a sweet impassioned hour,
  When not an eye was near,
To steal into my lonely bower,
  And kiss her image there.

Earth held not on its globe the man
  Who breathed that holy air;
No mortal eye but mine did scan
  My folly with my fair;
Sole monarch of that silent spot,
  All things gave place to me;
I did but wish—no matter what—
  Each obstacle would flee.

And did she love ?—she loved me not,
  But gave her hand away ;
I hied me to my lonely spot—
  In anguish, passed the day ;
And such a desolation wide
  Spread o'er that holy place,
The stream of life itself seemed dried,
  Or ebbing out apace.

But what I did—what madly said—
  I cannot tell to any—
Her portrait in its place hath staid,
  Though years have flown so many ;
Nor can each lovely lineament
  So deep impressed, depart,
Till Nature shall herself be spent,
  And thou shalt break, my Heart.

[For the Southern Literary Messenger.]

Mr. Editor,—I send you a Parody upon Bryant's Autumn, apparently written by some disconsolate citizen of Richmond, after the adjournment of the Legislature in time past. If the picture be faithfully drawn, it may perhaps amuse the members of the Assembly who are now in your city.

PARODY ON BRYANT'S AUTUMN.

The very dullest days are come, the dullest of the year,
When all our great Assembly-men are gone away from
    here ;
Heaped up in yonder capitol, how many bills lie dead,
They just allowed to live awhile, to knock them on the
    head ;
Tom, Dick and Harry all have gone and left the silent
    hall,
And on the now deserted square we meet no one at all—
Where are the fellows ? the fine young fellows that
    were so lately here,
And vexed the drowsy year of night with frolic and good
    cheer,

Alas! they all are at their homes—the glorious race of
    fellows,
And some perhaps are gone to forge, and some are at
    the bellows.
Old Time is passing where they are, but time will pass
    in vain;
All never can, though some may be, transported here
    again.
Old "what d'ye call him," he's been off a week or may
    be more,
And took a little negro up behind and one before.
But What's his name and you know who, they lingered
    to the last,
And neither had a dollar left and seemed to be down-
    cast;
Bad luck had fallen on them as falls the plague on men,
And their phizzies were as blank as if they'd never
    smile again;
And then when comes December next, as surely it will
    come,
To call the future delegate from out his distant home,
When the sound of cracking nuts is heard in lobby and
    in hall,
And glimmer in the smoky light old Shockhoe Hill and
    all,
An old friend searches for the fellows he knew the year
    before,
And sighs to find them on the Hill Capitoline, no
    more;
But then he thinks of one who her promise had belied,
The beautiful Virginia, who had fallen in her pride.
In that great house 'twas said she fell, where stands her
    gallant chief,
Who well might weep in marble, that her race had
    been so brief,
Yet not unmeet it was, he thought—oh no, ye heavenly
    powers!
Since she trusted those good fellows, who kept such
    shocking hours.

[For the Southern Literary Messenger.]

MR. EDITOR.—The following sketch was given me by one of those mail stage story-tellers, who abound on our roads, and enliven the drowsy passengers by their narratives. It is founded on fact, and may not be unacceptable to such of your readers as are fond of delineation of human character in all its variety of phases.

SALLY SINGLETON.

Who thundering comes on blackest steed,
With slacken'd bit and hoof of speed ?—*Byron.*

A horseman passed us at full speed, whose wild and haggard look arrested the attention of my friend. In the name of all that is singular, said he, who can that be, and whither is he posting with such rapidity ? His garb seems of the last century, and his grizzled locks stream on the wind like those of some ancient bard.

That man, replied I, is a lover, and is hurrying away to pay his devoirs to his mistress, who married another, and has been dead for many years.

"Indeed, you surprise me," he rejoined. "He has, it is true, the 'lean look' of Shakespeare's lover; the 'blue eye and sunken ;' the 'unquestionable spirit,' and 'every thing about him demonstrates a careless desolation'—yet I should have imagined, that the snows of so many winters had extinguished all the fires of that frosty caucasus : but tell me who he is and what is his story."

"His name is Wilson ; and that of the lady whom he loved was Sally Singleton. I would that I had the graphic power of Scott to sketch a tale of so much interest. If Sir Walter has immortalized an old man, mounted on his white pony, and going in quest of the tombstones, how much is it to be regretted that the same master hand cannot be employed to perpetuate the memory of yonder eccentric being, whose love lives on after the lapse of twenty years, in spite of the marriage and death of his mistress—in spite of the evidence of his own senses, and, notwithstanding every human effort to dispel his delusion. Regularly every morning, for the last twenty years, no matter what the state of the weather, (alike to him the hail, the rain, and the sunshine,) has he mounted his horse, and travelled a distance of ten miles, to see his beloved Sally Singleton. His custom is, to ride directly up to the window of her former apartment, and in a courteous manner to bow to his mistress, in token of his continued attachment. Having performed this act of gallantry, he waves with his hand a fond adieu, and immediately gallops back with a triumphant air, as if perfectly satisfied with having set his enemies at defiance. "The course of true love never did run smooth," and in this case, whether "misgrafted in respect of years," or "different in blood," or "standing on the choice of friends," is not exactly known; but the lady was wedded to another, and died soon after. Her lover would never believe in her marriage or her death. His mind, unhinged by the severity of his disappointment, seems to have retained nothing but the single image of her he loved, shut up in that apartment; and he resolved to brave every difficulty, to testify his unchanging devotion. Obstacles were purposely built across his path—the bridges were broken down—the idle boys would gather around him, and assail him in their cruel folly—guns, even, were fired at him,—all in vain! The elements could not quench the fervor of his love—obstacles were over-leaped—he swam the rivers—the boys were disregarded—balls could not harm him. He held a charmed life; like young Lochinvar,

> "He staid not for brake,
> And he stopp'd not for stone;"

but dashed onward to his beloved window, and then, contented with this public attestation of his unalterable love, returned with a look of triumphant satisfaction to his joyless home. As a last effort to remove the veil from his eyes, a suit was instituted, in which he was made a party, and proof of the lady's marriage and death was purposely introduced to undeceive him. He listened with cold incredulity to the witnesses; smiled derisively at that part of their testimony which regarded her marriage and death; and the next morning was seen mounted as usual, and bowing beneath the window of his adored Sally Singleton.

~~~~~~~~~~~~~~~

WASHINGTON AND NAPOLEON.

THE CONTRAST.

"Urged by a curiosity common to all strangers, Captain Locker-by visited the tomb of Bonaparte. The spot where the tomb stands is only accessible by ticket. It was railed round with green paling, and a sentinel walked round it night and day, to prevent approach within the railing."

Behold what a contrast is here!
  Two heroes gone down to decay—
The grave of the one, how deserted and drear!
  While the other is deck'd in its marble array,
  And a sentinel guards it by night and by day.

Oh what was the life of the first,
  That in death they have left him thus lone?—
Was the crown of the Tyrant his thirst?
  And mounting in blood on the steps of a throne—
  Had he murdered his thousands to aggrandize one?

Of grandeur of soul was there none
  In that bosom transform'd to the clod;
The end of its government done,
  To abandon the lictor, the axe and the rod,
  When it look'd on its nothingness—thought of its
    God?

But see what a far different scene!
  The tomb of the valiant and wise!
Encompass'd secure by its paling of green,
  And gleaming in white, as those tropical skies
  Beam down on the waste where St. Helena lies.

Lo! numbers resort to that spot,
  And beauty bows too at the shrine—
Oh virtue! how envied thy lot!
  The grave cannot darken thy splendor divine,
  Nor sully thy brightness, but adds to its shine.

Yet Christian!—come nearer and read,
  For conjecture hath led us astray—
Hast thou heard of one false to his creed?
  Of a blood-loving tyrant—ferocious—whose sway
  Was supported by rapine, while earth was his prey?

'Tis to him that these honors are paid,
  And his dust must be guarded—from whom?
Are the terrified nations afraid
  Lest he yet should arise from the curse of his doom,
  And bursting its cerements, escape from the tomb?

Ah no! he lies powerless now!
  But thousands would bear him afar:
To this Juggernaut long did they bow,
  And were abjectly crush'd by the wheels of his car,
  As triumphant he rode through the red fields of war.

Is virtue then nought but a name?
  Let us turn to the spot we have passed—
If guilt can exult in its shame,
  The good in his grave may be silently cast—
  Abandoned—unnoticed—the scene but a waste!

Yes, yes, thou art dumb with amaze—
  'Tis Washington slumbers below—
Was language too weak for His praise?—
  Was the grief so profound that it baffled all show,
  Or the feeling too deep for the utt'rance of woe?

Let us hope that it was—let us trust
  That we honor the Friend of Mankind—
That the Corsican despot in dust
  His merited meed of abhorrence shall find
  In the progress of truth and the march of the mind.

THE DYSPEPTIC MAN.

Mr. Editor,—I am so unfortunate as to be the wife
of a dyspeptic man, and shall find some relief if you
will permit me to spread my complaints upon the
pages of your Messenger. Men are "April when they
woo, December when they wed," as I have found to

my cost. My husband was once as tender and affectionate as I could wish, but, poor man, he is now totally changed; I suppose it is owing to his having the dyspepsia. He is so peevish and fretful, I hardly dare speak to him;

"He's always compleenin frae mornin to e'enin;"

and it is impossible to keep pace with the endless variety of his ailments. If I happen to make a mistake, and inquire after the wrong pain, he flies into a violent passion, and reproaches me for a want of sympathy in his sufferings. It was but yesterday I happened to say, "my dear, how is the pain in your back?" (I had forgotten it was his side.) This was enough; he cursed matrimony, and swore it was the vilest of all institutions; that a wife was nothing more than a legalized tormentor; that if he were single, he would not marry any woman under the sun—no, not if she had a bulse of diamonds torn from a Begum's ear, and much more in the same strain; and at last cooling down, he asked me if I did not remember that his last pain was a pain in the side; and then entered into such a history of his malady, that I sorely regretted I had opened my lips upon the subject. What right have we to worry other people thus with our maladies? I never tell mine to any but the doctor, because I know that nobody else listens, and I doubt very much whether he does half his time. If any one gives my husband the common salutation of, how d'ye do? oh dear, he begins at the beginning of his disease, [like an old gentleman of my acquaintance, who always begins at the Revolution,] and traces it down through all its variations for the last five years—tells all the remedies he has used, and their effects, until you may see a half suppressed smile lurking about the lips of the interrogator, which increases at length to so broad a grin, that I am in agony for the consequences. He has tried in turn every remedy of every quack upon earth, and has gone so far as to punch himself almost to death with his own fists, by the advice of one Halstead. At first he is always pleased with the medicine, but at the end of two or three days he protests that he is worse, much worse, and vents his spleen upon the physic, the inventor, and upon me for permitting him to use such vile trash. Sometimes he comes to me, and tells me exultingly that he has at last found out the panacea—the grand catholicon for all his sufferings. "My dear B——," he will say, "let me explain to you the philosophy of this matter. When food is taken into the human stomach, if it cannot undergo a proper digestion, it goes through the putrefactive process; just such a process as would take place in animal or other substances, if exposed to the action of heat and moisture in the open air: a quantity of carbonic acid gas is disengaged, and this gas filling the stomach, acts by mechanical pressure, and thus produces the pain I feel. Now I have discovered that in consequence of my habit of eating fast, my food is not sufficiently triturated, and of course the gastric juice [heaven help me!] cannot act upon it; and I am exactly in the situation of the sheep or any other ruminating animal, who swallows the herbage whole, and then regurgitates, that it may undergo a better mastication. Well, what then is the remedy? I will tell you; I will make John pound my food in a mortar, which will supply the necessary trituration and thus I shall be a well man." He sent off immediately to a druggist and purchased a nice little wedgewood mortar, and there stood John, every day, behind his chair, pounding his meat, bread and vegetables, into a revolting mass, until my poor ears were well nigh deafened with the shrill din of the pestle against the sides of the mortar. Was ever woman so beset? At the end of a week, finding himself no better, he threw the mortar, pestle and all, at John's head, and would certainly have pounded him to death, but for a fortunate dodge, which permitted the mortar to come in contact with my china press, where it made sad havoc among my most valuable ware. He was very glad, he said, because I had no business to let the press stand there. It was on the tip of my tongue to say, "bray a fool in a mortar," &c., but I checked the impulse, and mildly said, I was very sorry indeed, that he could get no re-

5*

lief. This somewhat mollified him, and the next day
he came to me and apologized for what he had done,
and promised to repair the damage by making me a
handsome present; but this calm was of short duration,
for he soon relapsed into gloom—and as he sat by the
fire, smoking his pipe, he all at once declared that it
must have been the cursed tobacco which had poisoned
his existence; that during the combustion of the tobac-
co an oil was disengaged, which, mixing with the
saliva, was taken up by absorption into his lungs, and
had eaten them to a honey-comb. John was immedi-
ately called: "Here," said he, "John take this pipe,
and d'ye hear, sir, hide it—hide it where I never can
find it again." John accordingly took the pipe, but
struggled in vain to choke his laughter. Before he
could escape from the room, he burst out into such a
loud, distinct, irrepressible ha! ha! that there was no
mistaking the thing, and he was soundly caned for his
involuntary breach of decorum. About three days
after this, in the evening after tea, my husband's fa-
vorite time for smoking, I observed him very restless,
indeed; he rose, walked about the room, sat down,
whistled, hummed a tune, and rose again. At last he
began to rummage about the wainscot and mantle-
piece, and behind the book-case, and suddenly turning
round he called John in a softened voice; "John, my
good fellow, where is my pipe? I must have left it in
the study; do go and look for it." John hesitated and
grinned. "What the devil is the fellow laughing at?
Begone, sir, and bring my pipe immediately." John
speedily vanished. Turning to me, "you see," said
my husband, "my unhappy condition; my very ser-
vants turn me into ridicule, and you do not reprove
them for it." I could not reply, but felt anxious to
point out to him that he could never hope to be well,
because he would not adhere for a space of time suffi-
ciently long to any plan whatever. His scheme now
is to eat nothing but cold bread. It must be set away
in a pure place to *ripen* as he calls it. Hot bread, just
from the oven, he says, is giving out carbon continually,
and has not imbibed a sufficiency of oxygen to make it

wholesome. Can you forbear smiling, my friend? Now I know there is nothing of literature in all this, unless the chemical disquisitions of my wretched husband may be so considered; but nevertheless I flatter myself you will give me a place in your Messenger, because many a victim of dyspepsia may look into this mirror, and see himself. BELINDA.

PICTURE OF OLD VIRGINIA.

> Look here upon this picture—and on this,
> The counterfeit presentment.—*Hamlet.*

Virginia had been beautiful
    And owned a lovely land;
Her sons, who were so dutiful,
    Went with her heart and hand;
They raised her to the highest seat,
    By talents and by worth,
And sent her name in accents sweet,
    Far ringing through the earth.

But lately she had fallen off;
    Her beauty was impaired;
Her younger sons were heard to scoff—
    They might at least have spared.
'Twas said that she was growing blind,
    Was lazy and supine,
And that she weakly lagged behind
    Her sisters, grown divine.

That all her days were spent, forsooth,
    In one eternal chime
About her deeds of early youth—
    "Resolves" of former time.
Naught could be said and nothing told
    But she more devils spied;
"More devils than vast hell could hold"—
    Or all the world beside.

And strangers* did her land deride—
   With wagging tongue, reviled;
Wild beast, they said, had multiplied
   In that most barren wild;
Her houses were untenanted—
   The fox† had *manned* her walls;
And *"rank grass"* waved around his head,
   As in old Ossian's halls.

Her moral strength and physical,‡
   Aye, both of them, were gone,
And every man seem'd phthisical,
   Or like to tumble down;
Her talents all were buried deep,
   Or in some napkin hid,
Or with the mighty dead, did sleep
   Beneath the coffin lid.

But far! oh far beyond all these,
   She had displeased her God;
Inter dolosos cineres,
   She on volcano trod;
She could not get of nights her rest;
   At midnight bell for fire,
She hugged her infants to her breast,
   Prepared for funeral pyre.

Virginia roused herself one day,
   And took her picture down;
And as she gazed, was heard to say—
   Am I thus hideous grown?

---

*See Col. Benton's description of Virginia, done into verse, beginning thus:
    "As Benton jogg'd along the road,
     'Twas in the Old Dominion,
    His thoughts were *bent-on* finding food
     For preconceived opinion," &c.

†"The fox peeped out of the window, and the rank grass waved around his head. Desolate is the dwelling of Moina—Silence is in the house of her fathers."—*Ossian.*

‡ Man's strength is gone, his courage—zooks!
And liberty's fine motions, &c.—*Benton.*

And am I stupid—lazy—blind—
  A monomaniac too !
Relaxed in body and in mind ?
  Oh no ! it is not true.

There lies outstretched my glorious land,
  With her capacious bay ;
My rivers rush on every hand,
  With sail and pennon gay ;
My mountains, like a girdle blue,
  Adorn her lovely waist,
"*And lend enchantment to the view,*"
  As in "*the distance*" traced.

I'll hie me straight to Richmond town,
  And call my liege men there ;
And they shall write these libels down,
  Or fill me with despair.
I have a friend, who'll make some stir,
  And take my work in hand ;
I'll send him forth my "Messenger"—
  To "*spy out all the land.*"*

That Messenger went gaily forth
  Throughout her old domain,
And there found many men of worth
  Would snatch their pens again ;
And since their mother's blood was up—
  To cast her odium by,
Would shed—of ink—their latest drop
  T' inscribe her name on high.

The land which he went out to sift
  No milk and honey floods—
It takes not two her grapes to lift†—
  But grapes festoon her woods.

* And Moses sent them to spy out the land of Canaan.

† And they came unto the brook of Eshcol, and cut down from thence a branch with one cluster of grapes, and they bare it between two upon a staff, * * * * * and they told him, and said, we came unto the land whither thou sentest us, and surely it floweth with milk and honey, and this is the fruit of it.

No want of food, for beast or man,
　　There met his eager gaze ;
Find better bacon !—greens !—who can ?
　　Or finer fields of maize !*

Her Tuckahoes, 'tis true, are slim.
　　And of a bilious hue ;
But then he found the Anakim
　　Beyond the mountains blue :
Some men he found in safety chains—
　　All crossed upon the breast—
They seem'd indeed to have no brains :
　　But these all lands infest.

The women look'd so passing fair,
　　How shall their charms be told ?
By their Iachimos† they were
　　Like brilliants set in gold.
Of such *pure water* was each maid ;
　　So sparkling unto view—
No wonder that it should be said
　　They never could turn *blue.*

No foxes here, peep'd windows through ;
　　But oft at early morn
They're seen to brush the glittering dew,
　　Pursued by hounds and horn :
Her *"hounds are of the Spartan breed"*—
　　"So sanded and so flew'd,"
All *"dewlap'd"* they, and all *"crook-kneed"*—
　　As Cadmus e'er halloo'd.

* In old Virginia, stint of food
　　Diseases have engender'd—
The mind is gone,—to want of blood
　　Good morals have surrender'd

Houses are fallen—fences down—
　　And men are now much scarcer—
Wild beasts in multitudes are known,
　　That every day get fiercer.

Flee gravel—grit—and heartless clay—
　　Nor corn nor oats will grow there—
To westward hie—away—away !
　　No heartless clay you'll know there.—*Benton.*

† The yellow Iachimo.—*Shakspeare.* (Cymbeline.)

In short, all zealots are run mad
    T' abuse this pleasing sod;
Where people sleep as sound, egad,
    As in the land of Nod:
What! colonize old coachman Dick!
    My foster brother Nat!
My more than mother, when I'm sick!
    "Come, Hal, no more of that."

EXTRACT FROM A POEM,

ENTITLED

OLD VIRGINIA GEORGICS.

"Quid faciat lætas segetes,
*   *   *   *
*   *   *   *
Hinc canere incipiam."

Argument.

Virginia husbandry and that depicted by Virgil contrasted—
ploughing—horses, and manner of driving—gear—mules—the
ox—pastures—harrows, skimmers, &c.—crab grass—shepherds—
sheep—rogues—runaways—wolves—hounds—milk—milk-maids—
fence rails—watlings—invocation—address to Arators—shallow
ploughing—clover—gypsum—cowtail—Sir Humphrey Davy—
year begins—clodhoppers—overseers—hiring day—bonds—distri-
bution of labor—grubbing—effects of leaving stumps—old fences—
hogs, &c., &c., &c.

I sing the tillage old Virginia knows,
Which cheats with hope the husbandman who sows;
Not such as Maro sung in deathless strains,
To piping shepherds and Italian swains.
With *"crops immense"** no *"barn here ever cracks;"*
The wheat comes always badly from the stacks,
The corn falls ever *"most immensely"* short
Of vague conjecture or of false report;
No *well-fed bullocks* drag the glittering plough,
But half starv'd horses, and the Lord knows how!

---

*Immensæ ruperunt horrea messes.—*Virgil.*

Their shoulders chafed by hames of naked wood,
Till downward streams regardlessly the blood;
Urged on incessantly by thundering whips,
Of shouting negroes, with their *haws* and *geeps;*
No well-fed bullocks—no, but stubborn mules,
Well matched in villainy with him who rules;
For as their sides resound, just heaven! with sticks,
They oft let fly the most tremendous kicks: .
Tho' Pompey punch them, and tho' Cæsar curse,
It serves no purpose but to make them worse.
Some Frenchman* said—"would you convince a fool?
As soon go kick in stable with your mule."
Sententious wit!—how forcible!—how true!
I daub the picture which at once he drew.
No well-fed bullocks—but the bare-boned ox,
That suffering martyr to inhuman knocks!
Condemned, tho' pining with the *hollow horn,*
To exist on fodder, but to eat no corn:
Repast too scanty!—in the furrow flat
The sufferer sinks—"*the creature was too fat.*"†
No smiling pastures spread inviting here,
But dry hot fields on every side appear;
A sultry scene, a dismal waste, alas!
Where man's great object is to kill the grass.
This, tho' attack'd with never ending blows
From harrows, skimmers, and from clattering hoes,
Will rise abhorrent on the farmer's view,
Like the fam'd monster which Alcides slew;
Crab grass deracinate, and turn your backs,
It starts like Hydra from repeated whacks.
No shepherds tune their reeds to idle rhyme,
For none have leisure for such waste of time;
In truth the sheep by no one here are watch'd,
Save rogues, who suffer if they can be catched:
Hound—wolf—or runaway he only deals
In closely dogging at their nimble heels.
Alas! poor flocks! Arcadia's pastoral ground.
Nor "*thyme*" nor "*cytisus*" can here be found;

* Montaigne, I believe.
† The common excuse of the buckskin for the death of an ox, occasioned by starvation.

*"Distended udders"** ne'er approach the pail,
But only udders which are sure to fail.
Cows, bagless—poor—protuberant in joints—
Yield milk in spoonfuls, or, at most, in pints.
What Meliboeus, or what Tityrus too,
Could make rich cheese† from milk of azure hue,
Drawn by Miss Blackamoor at early morn,
From things so famish'd that they've turned to horn?
No "sallows‡ blossom on the neighboring hedge"—
We use but fence rails which are split by wedge,
Or watlings dry, unsought by *"Hybla's bees,"*
Which can't suck honey from dead limbs of trees.
Oh Muse!—but, pshaw!—that's stale!—a joke—
What Muse, I prithee, should I here invoke?
Those maids of Pindus, in this Christian land,
Should not be called on for a helping hand;
Ah! sooner call to aid the rustic lay,
Chiefs grown conspicuous in this farming day—
Who rule in clubs, and stately there preside,
And mount their hobbies for a tedious ride;
Who write long essays in a style confused,
Themselves more culpable than those abused;
Those sage Triptolemi who wield the pen,
To show our fathers were misguided men,
Far, far inferior to their wiser sons;
Mere Goths and Vandals! or like barb'rous Huns,
Whose sway brought ruin on the fairest plains—
These lacking mercy, and those lacking brains.
Come, then, Arators of the modern school,
And be benignant to a rhyming fool;
Himself a farmer of that set, i'fegs,
Who rip the goose to get the golden eggs,
The stupid, blind, short-sighted band,
Who skim the surface and undo the land;
Who rear no clover on a thirsty soil,
For why?—it grows not to reward their toil

* Bis venit ad mulctram, binos alit ubere foetus
† Pinguis et ingratæ premeretur caseus urbi.
‡ Vicino ab limite sepes,
   Hyblæis apibus florem depasti salicti.

Who strew no gypsum, but absurdly rail,
And swear 'tis nothing to the old cowtail.
These are their follies—these their crying sins,
Despite the pamphlet of enthusiast Binns;
I own the charge, and cry myself, peccavi,
I read but follow not Sir Humphrey Davy.
Arise Clodhoppers! now begins the year,
Attend the business which demands your care.
Overseers all! whom Taylor dubs the *"Priests**
Of sad destruction," mount your bob-tail'd beasts,
Kept always fat, when other nags are poor,
Tho' fed on nothing from the corn-house floor.†
'Tis hiring day—and to each county court,
Those who have negroes will this morn resort.
Bid, boldly bid, and stretch your eager throats,
O'erbid your rivals, and then give your notes;
Fear not the consequence when months roll o'er,
You've pass'd your bonds—so think of them no more;
When that is done, Virginians' debts are paid,
Till courts of justice lend their tedious aid.
High minded men disdain these petty rubs,
They leave such settlements to legal scrubs;
Skinflints alone are ever punctual found,
And take their bonds in at the time they're bound.
This done—return to your respective homes,
Prepare your corn-fields ere the spring time comes;
Review your several troops of sooty blacks,
Make *wenches* grub and *fellows* wield the axe;
Watch well the former, for they often leave
The stump, insidious, in the soil they cleave,
And when the plough, at some more distant day,
Incautious strikes, lo! every thing gives way;
Share—beam—and chains, and eke the back-bands too,
And Sambo staggers as he utters whew!
Wield well the axe, and fell the groaning trees,
Ope wide the corn-fields to the cooling breeze;
Naught more contributes than the air, I ween,
To keep your cornstalks of a healthful green:

* Taylor's Arator.
† An assertion always made, but somewhat apocryphal.

Go round your fences and adjust the rails,
Insert new pieces where the old one fails;
Stop all the hog-holes, lest the treacherous snout
Should find these pass-ways to your corn-field out.
Too many hope by aid of yelping dogs,
To guard the corn field from *"infernal hogs;"*
They leave their fences in a state unsound,
Then comes the hog and *grunts* them to the ground;
They plant—rest from their labors—sleep—
These curst marauders through the hog-holes creep;
Led on, perhaps, by some gigantic boar,
What havoc spread they while the laborers snore.
The morning breaks—what work for them that morn!
The hogs!—the hogs!—the hogs are in the corn!!*
Ah! then and there are hurrying one and all,
Like Byron's picture of the Brussels ball.†
Men, dogs, and hogs, in one confused pell mell,
And many a dismal squeal, and many a deafening yell;
Some dog soon fastens on some luckless ear,
Awhile hangs growling, then lets go with fear;
Anon he seizes on his mangled prey;
The Parthian wheels, and fights, and flies away.
Hold him! and hold him! makes the welkin ring,
While round his head the rocks and brickbats sing.
At length the battle ends—the routed swine
Have reach'd the Rubicon—the neighb'ring line—
Away they go with many a joyous snort,
The master curses, but 'tis Sambo's sport.
Oh! dreadful scenes! renewed perhaps next day,
"Quorum pars fui," as every one may say.

* * * * * *

* * * Hiatus maxime deflendus.

---

* The hogs are in the corn-field! tus em boy, tus em boy,
  The hogs are in the corn-field! tus em boy, ho!
Here we find the origin of the above popular song in Virginia.

† Ah! then and there was hurrying to and fro,
  And gath'ring tears and tremblings of distress.—*Byron.*

PINKNEY'S ELOQUENCE.

Hear you this triton of the minnows?—*Coriolanus.*

"Yet Mr. Pinkney is not an eloquent man; he is convincing to be sure—and that is to be eloquent in one way; but he would be more, and fails." "Nothing can be further from eloquence, if by eloquence be understood any thing that is persuasive, beautiful, dignified or natural, than the declamation or reasoning of William Pinkney." "His best speeches are a compound of strength, feeble ornament, affected earnestness, and boisterous turbulent declamation." "But God never meant him for an orator; he has no property of mind or body—no not one, calculated to give dominion in eloquence."

As old Doiley says in the farce, when told that "gold in the balance of philosophy was light as phlogisticated air," this must be deep, for I don't understand a word of it. The above are extracts from a work, in which the author undertakes to deny to Mr. Pinkney, the praise of eloquence. No kind of composition confounds me more than criticism, and especially that sort which pretends to develope the characteristics of some distinguished orator. If one

> Should
> So get the start of the majestic world

as to "bear the palm alone," we feel a very natural curiosity to know what was his appearance, his manner, and peculiar style of eloquence; but alas! in the hands of the critic, he assumes so many shapes, that the imagination is absolutely bewildered, and we turn away in despair of finding out what the man was like. The critic, like the newspaper, contradicts himself at every step. One sentence tells us what another denies; and we rise from the perusal of his sketch jaded and worn out with the variety of contrariant ideas which have passed through our brains. I am no critic, and heaven forbid I should ever belong to that cold hearted fraternity; who more often pervert taste than improve it; but I cannot forbear contesting the truth of this writer's assertions, and declaring that he seems to me to be a Lilliputian about the body of a Gulliver.

It has been said of Demosthenes, "that he has been deservedly styled the prince of orators. His orations are strongly animated, and full of the impetuosity and ardor of public spirit. His composition is not distinguished by ornament and splendor. Negligent of the lesser graces, he seems to have aimed at the sublime, which lies in sentiment. His action and pronunciation are said to be uncommonly vehement and ardent. The Archbishop of Cambray gives him the preference to Cicero; against whom he makes the objection of too much ornament. According, therefore to this author, if William Pinkney was not an orator, it follows that Demosthenes was none; because their style of eloquence seems to have been alike in almost every particular, except that Pinkney aimed at ornament, of which Demosthenes had none and Cicero too much. If speeches, characterized by stupendous strength, and turbulent declamation, and convincing argument, are neither "persuasive, nor dignified, nor natural," then was not Demosthenes persuasive, nor dignified, nor natural, and of course he was no orator according to this definition. If ornament be a fault in Mr. Pinkney, he had it in common with Cicero; but perhaps the author may say that Cicero attained what Pinkney only aimed at. Hear him then again on the subject of ornament, so passionately loved by Mr. Pinkney. "Bring him in contact with a truly poetical mind, and his argument resembles a battery of colored fire-works, giving out incessant brightness and reverberation." It would seem then that ornament is not a common trait of his eloquence, but a glitter which is effected by attrition against poetical minds. It is then that he draws upon the inexhaustible stores of beauty laid up in his mind, gathered from the writings of Shakspeare and others, and retained by the force of a powerful memory. He has no fancy of his own, but uses the fancy of others. Then surely he is far superior to Demosthenes, whose eloquence was thought to border on the hard and dry; alike impetuous, vehement, stupendous and convincing with him, and superadding a relish for the beauties of poetry; not aiming at any ornament of his own, but contented with what suggested itself in illustration of his argument from the pen of others. Then how is he feeble in ornament? But again; if there be nothing of dignity or nature in Pinkney's reasoning, how is it discovered that his mind is "adamant clamped with iron," (a poor conception, and suiting the ideas of a blacksmith better than a belles-lettres scholar—for the iron adds nothing to our thoughts of the strength of adamant;) that it is "a collossal pile of granite, over which the thunders of heaven might roll," &c., &c. It is useless to quote the rest of the unmeaning fustian of the sentence. After all this avowal of stupendous strength of argument, we are told in a subsequent paragraph, that say what we will of Mr. Pinkney's argument, he the author, never saw him yet—no never, pursue his argument steadily for ten minutes at a time. Then how can it be so overwhelming and convincing? Nothing lessens so much the force of argument as a perpetual aberration from the subject. Again; "God never meant him for an orator, he has no property of mind or body," &c., &c. Not to say any thing of the presumption and impiety of determining for God, I would ask what are the bodily properties of an orator? This writer has not condescended to define them, although he dwells at large upon such as he thinks cast discredit upon Mr. Pinkney. It is scarcely necessary to observe that Demosthenes was ungraceful in figure and action; and that not only orators, but very wise and learned men have been repulsive in their persons, their features, and their manners also. Though Cæsar and Cicero were exempt from defect in this respect, as far as I remember, Demosthenes stuttered—Socrates was bald and flat nosed—Antony a rough soldier—Lord Chatham's eloquence was forcible, but uniform and ungraceful—Fox was a fop of Bond street, and wore high-heeled morocco shoes. Mr. Pinkney therefore may, without reproach, be a "thick, stout man, with a red fat English face," and Mr. Fox will keep him in

countenance as a fashionable man. The facetious
Peter Pindar has said, that

> Love hates your large fat lubberly fellows,
> Panting and blowing like a blacksmith's bellows ;

but I never heard that oratory did.

In the next breath we hear that "Mr. Pinkney has a
continual appearance of natural superciliousness and
affected courtesy." Continual—and yet afterwards, his
manner is exceedingly arrogant and unpropitiating ;
and his deportment has been already described as
"brutal, arrogant, full of sound and fury, accompanied
by the rude and violent gestures of a vulgar-fellow."
One moment he is a giant, not only metaphorically, but
in sober truth, if we may judge from his stentorian
lungs, which have caused the author's whole system to
jar—and from those violent gesticulations, which indi-
cate uncommon personal strength ; the next, he turns
out to be only five feet ten, and a petit maitre, and
affectedly courtly and conciliatory ; and yet "nothing
could make a gentleman of him ; he can neither look,
act, speak, sit, nor talk like one." Notwithstanding
all this scurrility and abuse of Mr. Pinkney's person,
the author is not yet exhausted, but lavishes more upon
his intellect. "The physical powers of Mr. Pinkney,"
he says, "are to my notion, strictly correspondent with
his intellectual ones, both are solid, strong and substan-
tial, but without grace, dignity or loftiness." Loftiness !
the same man who has such "prodigious elevation and
amplitude of mind," "and both have a dash of fat
English dandyism." I confess myself wholly at a loss
to comprehend what the fat dandyism of the intellectual
power is. A man's mind might, by a forced metaphor,
be said to be dandyish, perhaps ; but a *fat mind* is a
solecism in words wholly inadmissible, I think. "His
style of eloquence," it is added, "is a most disagreeable
and unnatural compound of the worst faults of the
worst speakers." "He is said to resemble Lord Erskine
as he was in the day of his power: it is a libel on Er-
skine, who was himself a libel on the reputation of his
country as a speaker." "The language of Mr. Pink-

ney does resemble that of Lord Erskine ; his reasoning is about as forcible." If the term style here be the manner of speaking appropriate to particular characters, I have shown that the censure is equally applicable to Demosthenes, the prince of orators, who, in addition to his vehemence, was so ungraceful in his motions, that it was necessary for him to practice with a naked sword hanging over his shoulder; and therefore to compare Demosthenes to Lord Erskine is a libel on Lord Erskine, himself a libel on his country, as a speaker and argal as Shakspeare says, Demosthenes is inferior to English orators. If, again, the word style means the manner of writing with regard to language, these sentences would involve a contradiction, and Mr. Pinkney is alike and unlike Lord Erskine at the same time ! Yet why do I talk of Demosthenes ? In the following sentences the author admits that Mr. P. copied too closely after Cicero and Demosthenes, "He desired to be eloquent; he thought of Demosthenes and Cicero, and his heart swelled with ambition." He remembered not that he was to be a lawyer, and that Demosthenes and Cicero were declaimers. He who should look to move a body of Americans in a court of justice by the best thundering of Demosthenes, would only make himself ridiculous." Very true; and this may certainly prove that Mr. Pinkney might have been a greater lawyer, by bending the whole force of his mind to that one pursuit; but it has nothing to do with the premises. The ground is here changed; this is not the point to be proved—not the *quod erat demonstrandum.* The point to be proved is not the propriety of displaying eloquence before a jury, but that William Pinkney was never meant by God for an orator; that he has no property of mind or body to make one. This is assuredly the scope of the extracts. Had Mr. P. not aimed at ornament, his ashes might have passed undisturbed by the author, who allows that he was decidedly the greatest *lawyer* in America, but is very angry that he was not the greatest in the world. In spite of all this, however, Pinkney "pursued his way like a conqueror, and had well nigh established himself as the high priest of eloquence in America." Why, what a stupid, blind, misjudging race we must be, to think of choosing a man for our high-priest of eloquence, whom God never meant for an orator, and who had no property, not one, of mind or body, for his business—and never to awaken from our folly until this writer tore the urim and thummim from his breast. "The giant," he says, "is gone down like a giant to the household of death," and there should at least have escaped the imputation of baseness which deserved shooting. How giants die, I pretend not to know; but imagine such giants die pretty much like other people; and it seems to me perfectly ridiculous to talk of a man's dying like a giant. At that awful hour, the littleness of the greatest genius is a subject of melancholy reflection. I will only add that I know nothing of this writer. If his object was to guard us against the mischievous effects of a false taste in eloquence, he cannot be angry with me for wishing to guard against the equally bad effects of a false taste in criticism.

ETYMOLOGY.

The inventor of a new word must never flatter himself that he has secured the public adoption, for he must lie in the grave before he can enter the Dictionary.—*D'Israeli.*

MR. EDITOR.—I am an odd old fellow, and fond of etymology, and frequently amuse myself with tracing to their roots, words in familiar use. Having been confoundedly puzzled of late by the term caucus, which is in every body's mouth, and not being able to satisfy myself as to its origin, I have determined to have recourse to you, and will be infinitely obliged to you or any of your readers for a solution of the difficulty. If it be true as D'Israeli says, that the inventor of a new word cannot be secure of its adoption by the public, for he must lie in the grave before he can enter the dictionary—the man who made the aforesaid word must be still living, though at a very advanced age. I rather suppose, however, that D'Israeli is mistaken, and that the inventor has been dead a long time, and lived to see the general adoption of his word, notwithstanding it has as yet no place in any dictionary that I have seen. Supposing it to be an English word, I consulted Walker, and was mortified to find that he took no notice of it. I then made sundry combinations of other terms, but could light upon none that seemed at all plausible, except the word *calk* us, which, united into caucus, may produce a kind of onomatopœia, descriptive of the assemblage in question ; for to calk, is, according to the above mentioned lexicographer, "to stop the leak of a vessel," and inasmuch as a caucus is urged by the admirers of Mr. Van Buren, to be the means of stopping all leaks in our political vessel, there seems to be some show of reason in this derivation. Upon further reflection, however, I concluded that the word must be Greek, and having recourse to Schrevelius, found the paronymous term *kakos,* malus. This I presently rejected, though apparently descriptive of the pernicious tendency of caucus, because the institutors of that pestilent oligarchy would hardly have selected so barefaced an epitheton, such a cacophony, if I may so speak. On further search, upon meeting with kaukis, I was so much delighted with the near resemblance of sound, as to jump up and cry out "eureka ;" but moderated my rapture on discovering that "genus calceamenti," the explanatory terms in Latin, could not be tortured to any manner of application, unless indeed it was intended to indicate that the members of a caucus would be willing to stand in the people's shoes, upon the occasion of electing a president of the United States ; or unless we observe further the aliter baukos, jucundus, for it is literally a very pleasant and right merry way of getting rid of the difficulty of a choice by the people. So far the Greek. As to the Latin, I have consulted every dictionary in my possession, from Ainsworth and Young, up to old Thoma Thomasius, printed coventriæ Septimo Idus, Februarii, 1630, and can find nothing resembling our caucus, but the three-headed robber cacus, who by paronomasia, might be considered as the grand prototype of that modern monster, which has stolen, if not the cattle, at least the property of the American Hercules, and will keep it unless he rise in his might, and crushing the political thief resume his original rights. Now, Mr. Editor, I am disposed to rest here; though not quite so well satisfied as Jonathan Oldbuck was about the locality of Agricola's camp, from those mysterious initials which the mischievous Edie Ochiltree so wickedly interpreted to mean "Ailic Davy's lang ladle," and not "Agricola dicavit llhens lubens," as Monkbarns would have it;—but do observe, sir, the singular coincidences between cacus and caucus; the one a three-headed rogue—the other a sort of political Cerberus; the first slily taking away the cattle of another—the second insidiously cajoling the people of their rights; the former hiding them in a cave, where they were discovered by their bellowing—the latter betrayed by a bellowing from Maine to Georgia; and finally cacus demolished by Hercules, and caucus easily demolished by the Herculean force of public sentiment.

I acknowledge, however, that I am not entirely satisfied, notwithstanding this "confirmation strong," and hope you will speedily relieve the perplexity of

Your most obedient servant.

P. S. A friend facetiously suggests that caucus is nothing more than a corruption,—Caucus, quasi corkus; that is, shut close the doors that nobody may hear us.

THE GIRL OF HARPER'S FERRY.

Ah! tell me not of the heights sublime,
  The rocks at Harper's Ferry,
Of mountains rent in the lapse of time—
  They're very sublime—oh very!
I'm thinking more of the glowing cheek
  Of a lovely girl and merry,
Who climb'd with me to yon highest peak—
  The girl of Harper's Ferry.

She sailed with me o'er the glassy wave,
   In yonder trim-built wherry;
Shall I ever forget the looks she gave,
   Or the voice which rang so merry?
To the joy she felt, her lips gave birth—
   Lips, red as the ripest cherry—
I saw not Heaven above, nor Earth—
   Sweet girl of Harper's Ferry!

We clamber'd away over crag and hill
   Through places dark and dreary;
We stooped to drink of the sparkling rill
   And gather the blushing berry;
Dame Nature may sunder the Earth by storms
   And rocks upon rocks may serry,
But I like her more in her fragile forms,
   My girl of Harper's Ferry.

I followed her up the *"steps of stone,"*
   To where the dead they bury;
On Jefferson's rock she stood alone,
   Looking on Harper's Ferry—
But I, like Cymon, the gaping clown,
   Stood, lost in a deep quandary,
Nor thought of the river, the rock, the town,
   Dear girl of Harper's Ferry.

She carv'd her name on the well known rock,
   The rock at Harper's Ferry;
You would not have thought me a stone or stock,
   Bending o'er charming Mary—
Insensible rock! how hard thou wert,
   Hurting her fingers fairy,
Deeper she writ upon my soft heart—
   The girl of Harper's Ferry.

Ye who shall visit this scene again,
   This rock at Harper's Ferry,
Come pledge me high in the brisk champaigne,
   Or a glass of the palest sherry—
And this is the name which ye shall quaff,
   The name of Mary Perry!
She's fairer than all your loves by half—
   The girl of Harper's Ferry.

MODERN TRAVELLING.

Forty years ago I was a great traveller, and was pretty well acquainted with the means of transportation then in use; but about that time, I retired to the country, and settled upon a small farm, where I have, until lately, pursued the even tenor of my way. During the last summer, some business compelled me to set out for a distant point, and I left my little home with extreme reluctance. As I was to travel in a world about which I knew but little, except through the newspapers, I thought it right to rig myself out in somewhat better style than usual, so I put on my best *bib* and tucker, and repaired to town and sought a barber's shop to get my hair cut, and my beard shaved, humming as I went along the old song,

"I called to the barber, come shave me boy, do you hear,
And I'll give you sixpence for to spend in ale or beer;
Shave me, shave me, barber come shave me,
Make me look neat and spruce that Molly may have me."

Sixpence quotha! it cost me four-and-sixpence, at the least. When I opened the door, I was so much astonished at the elegance of the apartment, that I drew back, and would have retired, thinking I had made some mistake, when two or three fellows flew out upon me, and began brushing my coat with such impetuous violence that I could not escape from them; indeed it was with much ado that I could prevent my ears from being brushed off by their whizzing brooms. I was as restive, you may depend upon it, as my horse is under a cedar broom; twice they struck me severe blows on the cheek, but always begged pardon, so I could not be offended; and, indeed, I had made up my mind when I left home, not to betray my ignorance of present customs. All this time two small *shavers* were dusting my boots, and I protest it was with much difficulty I could keep my legs. After considerable suffering on my part, and repeated declarations of my being satisfied with their services, and paying each of them something, (for I saw they expected it,) they desisted.

7

I now expressed a wish to be shaved and trimmed, and was immediately disrobed, and ushered to a high-backed chair, where my head was roughly thrown back, my chin tucked, and the operation of shaving performed in the *"twinkling* of an *ejaculation."* It did not take long to cut my hair and strangle me with cologne water; but what was my surprise, when they were done with me, to find the whole of my occiput as bare as the palm of my hand, and nothing left upon my head but a few straggling locks at the side, time having already stripped naked my forehead. I was sadly vexed, but what could I say? I had voluntarily put myself in their power, and was devoutly glad when I got into the street, that I had escaped alive from their hands. Well, I had now paid four-and-sixpence; I had lost all my hair; my face had been scratched by brooms and lacerated by a razor, and I had learned in exchange that barbers were different folks now-a-days from what they used to be, and that men were brushed down like horses—rather a bad speculation! I had not been in this world, it is true, "ever since King Pepin was a little boy," but I was pretty old, and had never been treated so unceremoniously in my life. I had imagined when I entered the house, that I was going into just such a shop as my old friend Kippin used to keep, who received me with the profoundest of bows, and shaved me with a solemnity of manner that suited my temper exactly. No tawdry ornaments hung upon the walls; no mirrors flashed wheresoever you turned; no newspapers lay scattered around; no Helen Jewetts or other engravings caught your eye. His walls were mute as "Tara's Halls"—a piece of broken looking-glass stood upon the table, and an old shaving-can, encrusted with the smoke of a thousand fires, sat disconsolately in the chimney; but, nevertheless, these modern fellows cannot shave as Kippin *"used to could."* There is too much hurry in every thing now-a-days! It is true shaving must be done by steam—the water ought to be hot, but the razor travels too incontinently fast, and the whirlpools in my beard cannot be crossed over with such despatch—but, pshaw! this is nothing to what I have to tell of the changes in this world. My first trip was to be made in a steamboat which was to start (*fly* perhaps would be a better word) at ten o'clock at night. I had never been in one, having been of the same opinion with old What's-his-name, who never could be induced to go on board, not even when the boat was lying at the wharf without a particle of fire—when urged to go, and told that there was no earthly danger, he always shook his head doubtingly, and declared "there was no knowing what accidents might happen." However, go I must; my business required despatch, and there was no mode of travelling so expeditious. Accordingly, I went on board, and passing the fire-room, where they were just *firing up*, I stopped with unfeigned horror, and asked myself, if indeed I was prepared to die! I almost fancied myself at the entrance of the infernal regions, and the firemen, all begrimed and black and covered with sweat, seemed like the imps of the devil, tossing the damned spirits into the flames. I shuddered and turned away, inwardly vowing if heaven would be graciously pleased to spare me this time, I would never again voluntarily put myself in the way of being burnt to death. I proceeded to the cabin, which I found, as yet, unoccupied, and you may be certain if the barber's shop had surprised me, my amazement was now complete, at finding myself in the most splendid apartment I had ever beheld. I shall not attempt any description, because I have no doubt, Mr. Editor, you have seen many a one; all I shall say is, that having examined every thing with as much wonder as did Polyglott when "he dinner'd wi' a lord," I laid myself down in a berth, and could not satisfy myself of my personal identity, any more than could *he* who once went to see some great man, and was treated with so much distinction, that when he retired to bed, he lay some time revolving all that had passed, and the scene around him, and exclaimed, "can this be me." Putting his foot out of bed, (he had a remarkable foot,) egad! he cried, that is certainly my foot. Just so, clapping my hand to the back of my head, and feeling that the barber had nearly scalped me, I became assured that it was indeed your humble servant, and was trying to compose myself, when I heard a cry of "the stage is come," and in a few moments in walked the captain and seated himself at his writing-table, and immediately afterwards forty passengers, at least, rushed into the cabin, all talking in the loudest key, and dressed in every variety of mode, and seeming to strive with one another who should get first to the captain to pay his money. What does this mean? thought I; wherefore such hurry? "Why need they be so forward with death, who calls not on them?" as Falstaff says. I soon found out the cause; they were securing their berths, and as they passed mine, they severally peeped into it; at length, one prying more earnestly than the others, exclaimed, "halloo, my hearty, you are in the wrong box; you must come out." I made no reply, and he repeated his command to me to turn out—still I said nothing, and he turned to the captain: "I say, captain, here's a Jackson man in my berth." "Yes," said I, feeling my dander rise, as honest Jack Downing says, "and I shall assume the responsibility of staying in it." Alas! I reckoned without my *host*, for the captain came up and desired me to evacuate the premises. "Why," said I, "captain, I thought possession was eleven points of law." "None of your nonsense, sir," returned he, and took hold of my arm. Seeing how matters stood, I fixed myself Dentatus-like, with my back to the side of the boat, and seizing my hickory stick, defended myself manfully, but numbers prevailed over valor, and I was at last ignominiously dragged forth, like Smith from Chickahominy Swamp, to the no small amusement of the company, some of whom hurraed for old baldpate. Here was a pretty commencement of my journey! In the end, I was compelled to sleep upon a table, think o' that! and imagine my horror when I found myself stretched out like a corpse, with a sheet over me!! All my previous fears of being scalded to death rushed upon my mind, and I made sure that this was indeed my winding sheet. The thumping of the boat; the groans of the lever above, leaping and pitching like some vast giant struggling to be free; the snoring and snorting around me; the intense heat, produced by the juxta-position of so many human bodies, effectually banished sleep from my eyelids; I was "in a state of dissolution and thaw," and wished myself any where else, even in "the Domdaniel caves under the roots of Ocean," if there were such a place, so that I could escape my present thraldom. How often have I won- dered, said I to myself, that people could be so fool- hardy as to live at the foot of Mount Ætna or Vesuvius, where they are liable to be overwhelmed in a moment by burning lava; and here am I, lying near the crater of a volcano, without the hope of escape if there should be an eruption!! Overwhelmed by the oppressive weight of my thoughts, I sunk, from absolute exhaus- tion, about day-break, into a doze, from which I was almost immediately aroused by a bell, which I mistook for the last trump, and springing up perceived that it announced our arrival at the place of destination, and I was forced to huddle on my clothes as fast as possible. Such a scene of confusion and hurry as now presented itself, baffles my poor powers of description. Passen- gers, porters, trunks, wheel-barrows, hackmen, every body and every thing, in one moving mass upon the wharf, so completely confounded the few brains I had, that I stood like a fool, while "hack, sir?" was bawled in one ear, "hack, sir?" in another—"omnibus, sir? do you go in the omnibus?" One pulled me by the right, another by the left, until my limbs were almost dislocated. At last, remembering a little of my Latin, I concluded it must be right to go with all, and I cried out "omnibus!" "Your baggage, sir, where is it?" "God only knows, my friend," said I. "Is this it, sir?" "Yes, yes." Into the omnibus they shoved me, with such despatch, that had I been the *stout gentleman* himself, I am sure none could have seen even the "broad disk of my pantaloons." It was the first time in my life that I had ever travelled in a carriage without shutting the door, except once, upon compulsion, when my horses ran off with me; but if you will credit me, sir, there is no door to an omnibus; so I suppose omnibus

7*

means without a door, but in what language is more than I pretend to know. Perhaps it may be the Garamna language, but none but the author of the Doctor can tell that. If you should be acquainted with the tongue, Mr. Editor, just drop me a hint in your next number, and I shall be much obliged to you.

Well, praised be heaven, I had escaped the death of a hog, and felt somewhat revived by the morning air. Away we whirled with great rapidity to the rail-road depot, where the cars were ready to receive us. We were told that from some irregularity, I never knew what, we were to be drawn for some miles by horses, and I blessed my stars at the occurrence, as I had been anticipating, with some dread, that wonderful velocity of the engines of which I had heard and read so much; but short-lived indeed was my joy, as it began to be a matter of interesting speculation whether the cars meeting us, might not, peradventure, be driven by steam. We had not proceeded far, before our apprehensions were realized. Just as we turned an abrupt curvature in the road, there *came* the engine roaring and snorting upon us!! Mr. Editor, I have been pursued in my time by a mad bull; I have been upon the point of being tossed upon his horns; I have been in imminent peril of being run over by squadrons of wild horses, which had taken the stampado; I have seen perils by sea and perils by land, but never had I felt such alarm, such destitution of all hope of escape, as now. Our driver sprang from his seat, and had just time to unhitch his horses, but what were we to do? One man jumped out and broke his leg, the rest of us kept our seats. I could not leave mine—I was transfixed with horror—my eyes were starting from my head, and my mouth wide open. Breathless, we awaited the shock, and soon it came like a thunder-crash. What happened to others I cannot tell. All I remember distinctly is, that the concussion was so tremendous, that it brought my two remaining teeth so violently together, that they were both knocked out; they were the last of the Capulets, and I would not have taken a thousand dollars apiece for them; it is a wonder I did not die of fright—my hair, if I had any, must have turned gray ; but thanks to the barber, I had none. I was taken up more dead than alive, and nothing could induce me to hazard my life again. I consigned to the devil, all cars, steamboats, rail roads, their projectors and inventors, solemnly vowing never to be in a hurry again as long as I lived, but to remember the old maxim, *festina lente*—make haste slowly.

My business I abandoned in despair,—bought the dullest horse I could procure—sold my trunk, and got a pair of saddle-bags, and resolved to jog slowly and safely homeward. After a fatiguing journey, I reached my own house, where nobody knew me. When I told my wife who I was and what had occurred to me, she said it was a judgment upon me for being such a fool as to cut my hair in *that* fashion. She will never listen to me now when I attempt to repeat the particulars of my excursion, and that is the reason I have concluded to trouble you with my history. If it should entertain you, and serve as a warning to my countrymen not to be in such a confounded hurry in doing every thing, I shall be repaid for my trouble. The whole world seems to me to be in a sort of nèck-or-nothing state ; all the sobriety, frugality and simplicity of our forefathers seems to be forgotten, and the only object is, to grow rich suddenly, and time and space must be annihilated in the pursuit.

I am, sir, very respectfully, your most obedient, humble servant,

SOLOMON SOBERSIDES.

DEBATE ON THE CROW BILL,

In the Senate of Virginia, February 9th, 1826.

Crows and Choughs that wing the midway air,
Show scarce.—*Shakspeare.* (King Lear.)

MR. McCARTY.

By that bill, Mr. Speaker, 'tis meant to propose
The form of a law for the killing of crows;
A county requests us—the county Fairfax,
To place it as one in the list of our acts—
I'm sure, Sir, that you and that every one knows
How *very* destructive to corn are the *crows;*
There *is* not perhaps any bird, Sir, that hops,
That pulls up as much of the cornplanter's crops;
They gather by thousands and tear with their bills
Each plant as it peeps through the top of the hills;
I see, Sir, this subject produces some mirth,
But let not a crow, Sir, remain upon earth.
If the West is to pay for the wolf and its whelps,
Why may not the east for the crow or its scalps?
I hope then, the senate will pass, Sir, the law,
We wish not in Fairfax to hear a crow—caw.

MR. RUFFIN.

Mr. Speaker, I move to amend the crow bill
By adding to those who have license to kill—
Insert after Fairfax the words "Isle of Wight,"
"Southampton and Surry," you also may write.
'Tis not that I have—oh no, heaven knows,
A thirst, Mr. Speaker, for blood of the crows,
Prince George and the crows are on very good terms,
We want them to eat up that pest, the cut worms,
But some of my counties complain with Fairfax
And is'nt it right they should come in for snacks?

Mr. McCarty.

With this bill, Mr. Speaker, some wags down below
Are strongly suspected of *"picking a crow,"*
Against that amendment, I therefore shall vote,
We might just as well catch the *bill* by the *throat* ;
'Twill excite such a laugh in a certain great hall,
They'll scout from the House the amendment and all,
I hope, Sir, the bill will be then let alone,
This amendment will cause it to die with a *groan*.

Mr. Page.

Mr. Speaker ! ! ! I hope the amendment and bill
Will find in the Senate no jot of good will—
To hold out a bounty in any such case
Is simply rewarding the vagrant and base ;
From labor productive, 'tis taking away, Sir ;
Your hundreds to idle and waste all the day, Sir ;
Instead of promoting the true *wealth of nations*
'Tis taking men off from their suitable stations,
From digging—from grubbing and other hard blows,
To shooting their guns at a parcel of crows.
But, Sir, I assert it—'tis true on my word,
The crow is in fact a carniverous bird ;
He does'nt *like* corn, Sir—he would'nt eat grain,
He'd strut by the thing in a fit of disdain ;
If he only could get flesh enough for his turn,
What you think is his passion, he'd caw at and spurn ;
'Tis mere "Hobson's choice," with him when his scorn
Is seen to relax, and he gobbles your corn.
I would ask too the member who urges this tax,
If it be not unwise in the county Fairfax ?
If the end is effected, this crow bill enforces,
What *is* to become of *his mass of dead horses*?

Mr. Cabel.

It may seem, Mr. Speaker, to some of the counties
To be a small matter, this granting of bounties,
But long have I thought, Sir, 'twould be very wise
In planters, some plan of the kind to devise.
The interests of husbandry, calling now louder,
Must have something stronger than smell of gunpowder;

These birds come upon us like hordes, Sir, of Huns,
And take care to keep out of range of our guns;
Some people have tried a contrivance we know
Which all have consented to call a scare-crow;
But I've seen 'em light on it with great *nonchalance*
And hopping about as if learning to dance.
A plan I once thought of, I'll freely disclose,
'Twas to grant, Sir, a *pension* to each of these crows,
If I gave them as much of my corn as they'd eat
I thought that to steal it. would not be so sweet;
But alas, Mr. Speaker, they'll just as soon go
To the corn you have planted as that which you strew,
I own, Sir, a farm in the old Northern Neck,
Where crows would outnumber the grains which they
     peck,
And unless some provision is made in our laws,
I fear, Sir, the planter must give up his cause.

MR. RUFFIN.

Although, Mr. Speaker, I moved that three counties
Should also partake of these *ruinous* bounties,
I did it alone from a sense of my duty,
And not that I saw in the scheme any beauty.
What the gentleman said who was last on the floor,
In the truth of my *dogmas*, but rivets me more;
The plan of a pension we've heard him rehearse
Has proved like the *poor laws* an infinite curse.
His system, Sir, failing, conclusively shows
It swells but the number of paupers and crows;
Malthus and others have proved that such laws
Increase but the cramming of *bellies* and *craws*,
I therefore shall vote, Sir, against the whole bill,
And I wish that the Senate would help me to kill.

MR. JOHNSON.

That bill, Mr. Speaker, proposes to *tax*
All those who reside in the county Fairfax,
The *grower* of corn and he who grows *none* :—
'Tis *wrong*, Sir, injustice like this should be done.

Mr. Fry.

A law about wolves, Mr. Speaker's been made,
And a tax on the county requesting it, laid,
The man who *grows* wool and the man who does *not*
Are surely involved in a similar lot.—
The principle here is the same, Sir, I trow,
If you tax for the wolf you may tax for the crow.

Mr. Sharp.

A *single* remark, Mr. Speaker,—the man
Who does'nt make corn, eats bread if he can :
The more that is made, the cheaper he buys,
Then does'nt he profit when any crow dies ?

The Speaker arose from his arm chair at last
And ask'd if the bill in his hand should be passed,
And the "ayes" seem'd to have it, he said, by the sound
And the foes of the crows, how they crowd on the
      ground ! !

February 10th.

We hasten to notice an error we fell in,
Reporting this bill, as regards Mr. Allen.
That gentleman moved an amendment, to wit,
If laws on the subject were thought at all fit,
Those laws should be general, and each county court
In its wisdom, to scalping of crows, might resort;
He thought that a body so grave as the Senate
Should not have a thing like a crow bill within it ;

If the bill should go through with its one sided features,
Then year after year we should hear of these creatures;
'Twas best in his judgment to deal such a blow,
As would shut up forever the bill of the crow,
And this was the speech which gave Mr. Ruffin,
What Fairfax would call, a fit of "*humgruffin.*"
"He had no objection he said to the bill—
As regards other counties—enact what you will;
But as for his county, he warmly protested
By bell, book, and candle, if crows were molested,
The worms there would fearlessly riot and revel.—
All chance of the crop would be sent to the devil."

THE PETITION OF THE CROWS.

At a very numerous meeting of crows in the Northern Neck, assembled not for the purpose of opposing the election of General Andrew Jackson or John Quincy Adams, to the presidency, but to take into consideration the state of the crows, the following petition to the Legislature was vociferously adopted.

CORVUS CARNIVOROUS, *in the Tree.*

CROWOVER CORNHILL, *Scratchetary.*

To the Honorable Speakers and Members of the General Assembly of Virginia:

The petition of the crows of the Northern Neck, humbly complaining, sheweth unto your honors that your petitioners view with feelings of the deepest alarm, the various enactments of the legislature against them; they could have borne, without speaking, the injuries heretofore inflicted, because they were of a *partial* nature, and did not seem to contemplate the total eradication of their species, but now that they find from a *birdseye* view of your journal, that the war to be waged against them is one of entire extermination, they cannot forbear to cry out and respectfully ask of your honors what they have done, more than many other animals, to call down a vengeance so cruel and unrelenting. Not only are we exposed to death in a thousand shapes from poisonous preparations and villainous gunpowder, but recently with a refinement of malignity disgraceful to a christian people, grains of corn have been strung with horse hair, and your unfortunate petitioners, while attempting to swallow these affronts have been subjected to phthisical tortures of a character wholly indescribable. Not satisfied with punishments so entirely disproportioned to our offences, your honors have sanctioned by law, that *aboriginal abomination* of *scalping,* against which, when practised on yourselves, your outcries have been loud and unceasing. Is it not enough that our domestic privacy is rudely violated, and our lovely little ones mercilessly torn from us in spite of their cawing, while we ourselves are assailed on every side by the engines of death, but our miserable bodies must be savagely mangled, and our scalps exhibited to your magistracy contemptuously strung upon strings rattling in horrible aridity!! To say nothing of the demoralizing effects of such exhibitions, and the impolicy of destroying so useful a race as ourselves, for proof of which we beg leave to refer your honors to Wilson's Ornithology; permit us to ask why are we singled out as the objects of your vengeance, when nothing is said of the rat or squirrel, the first more destructive than ourselves, and the last so much so as to have given birth to that most sarcastic observation of the Hon. John Randolph of Roanoke, viz. "that the Northern Neck resembles the outside row of a corn-field, where the squirrels had already commenced their nibbling;" a language so prophetical and seemingly so verified by recent events, that we, sagacious as we are known to be, are astonished at his sagacity. On this subject we content ourselves with the simple observation of *verbum sap.* which is better Latin, we venture to say, than "*ignæ fatuæ.*" Thanks to the fabulists, who have taught us all languages, and here we cannot refrain from remarking that certain orators appear to have been "at a great feast of the languages," but to have come away without even "the scraps." That more substantial participation in "the flesh pots" may be hereafter exhibited, we pretend not to know anything about, and hasten to call your attention to other matters, more relevant to our present petition.

No longer ago than at the last session of your Assembly, the hog, at the bare mention of the destructiveness of which the Virginia farmer ought to tremble, was treated with a courtesy which, when contrasted with the cruelty evinced to us, is truly astonishing. He was absolutely presented with the freedom of the town of Lewisburg, not in a golden box, but upon parchment, and permitted to rove at large, exempt from all restraint, that he might be upon a footing with the rest of his fellows throughout the state. It surely cannot be unknown to your honors that the hog is, beyond all contradiction, the most destructive to grain of all animals upon earth. In a single night he will ravage an entire field, and notwithstanding the authority to do so, derived from your honorable body, his bloody laurels often attest the sanguinary combat he has waged in defence of his privileges. To statesmen so experienced as yourselves, it would be presumption in us to call your most serious attention to the absurdity of conferring such honors upon an animal so voracious and so regardless of the true *wealth* of *nations.* In the single article of fencing, one-third of the labor annually employed in this state might be dispensed with if this licensed freebooter, this swinish corsair, were subjected to imprisonment. It is true we may be reproached with being frequently seen perched upon his back, and we sincerely wish that we could ride into power upon his shoulders, as many of the race of man have done upon the shoulders of their fellows ; but alas! like the innocent apple upon the head of the son of Tell, the deadly shaft pierces us through, while the hog moves on unharmed, the pride and favorite of republicans. It is far from the wish of your petitioners to say one word that has reference to political matters. It is certainly our interest to please both sides—we have made "geoponicks" rather than politics our study, and notwithstanding we possess in an eminent degree that craft which is the distinguishing trait of the profound politician, the necessity of procuring subsistence has driven us rather to the contemplation of corn-hills than codes. Nevertheless we find ourselves constrained to say that we are somewhat in the predicament of Gen. Jackson. His deeds have been *long known, commented* upon, *triumphantly vindicated,* and yet there are some who seem to have been in a sort of political lethargy, and to have suddenly awakened to a keen perception of his atrocities. The flood long pent up in their bosoms hath at length found a vent, and a torrent of vituperation has poured down upon his head, so sweeping and so overwhelming that no place of security can be found for the hero of New Orleans, save the strong walls of your penitentiary. Now,

> "Ever since old Adam was made,
> Pulling of corn has been our trade"—

and yet, with this knowledge on your part, vengeance hath slept until lately; the *plea* of *necessity* has been our justification—we have acted, as Mr. Adams says, under a higher sanction than human laws, and yet nothing short of an ignominious end will satisfy the enemies of our advancement. Nor are we at a loss to find a parallel in our case to that of Mr. Adams, if that eminent scholar will permit us to compare the humble Mantua with lofty Rome. Like him, we fondly flattered ourselves that our nests, carefully cemented by the aid of Clay, were too securely reared toward the skies to be reached by our opponents. We did not dream that *explorations* would produce so much mischief; we hoped that in these *observatories* we might securely sit, and that any attempt to disturb us would be *"ineffably stupid,"* when lo! the *auri sacra fames,* (more Latin, an' please your worships,) the cursed love of treasury pap, has suddenly overturned all our hopes and left us a prey to despair. We forbear to trespass longer upon your valuable time, although this subject is capable of great amplification, and conclude with an earnest prayer that your honors will reject, promptly and with merited scorn, every *bill* which has for its object the further wounding of your petitioners, and if this humble boon be too much to grant, we implore that you will in mercy allow us at least the writ of *habeas corpus,* and ordain that our mangled crowns shall be no longer, with Indian ferocity, exhibited to your magistracy, an indecent spectacle and barbarian trophy, but that each victim, *in propria persona,* shall be produced, and your petitioners will ever pray, &c. &c.

Signed by

MANY CROWS.

THE CAPITOL.

Quoth I, with a' my heart I'll do't,
  I'll get my Sunday sark on,
An' meet you on the holy spot;
  Faith, we'se hae fine remarkin.
                          Burns' Holy Fair.

Old Richmond bell began to groan,
  The deafen'd year a greeting :
And loud proclaim'd the hour o' noon,
  The House's hour o' meeting—
The sun was bursting through the clouds
  That wrap the smoky city,
And men were thronging forth in crowds
  And all the women pretty,
      So gay, that day.

As lonesomely I took the street,
  To breathe the genial air,
A laughing friend I chanced to meet,
  Quite gay and debonair—
He press'd my hand with friendly grip,
  True index of the soul,
And said, come take with me a trip,
  To our great Cap—i—tol,
      For fun, this day.

I will with all my heart, quoth I,
  Since there I ne'er have been,
But first, my friend, pray tell me why
  This rushing out and in—
Has Richmond City seen old *"Scratch?"*
  Or are *State Rights* in danger ?
That folks move on with such despatch,
  You see I'm but a stranger
      To things, this day.

Oh no, quoth he, a better joke
  By far than that we crack,
They've killed a man called Roanoke,
  Whose christian name was Jack;

A woman threw a tile of yore,
  And smote some fellow's head,
But Jack was smit by something more,
  A Tyler killed him dead,
      Quite dead, one day.

That Tyler now is also dead,
  And turned 'tis said to Clay,
And so we go to choose, instead,
  Some man to bear the sway—
The troops of those who wish to reign,
  Will fight like bold Macduff;
The shout will be with might and main,
  "Lay on" and he who *"cries enough"*
      "Be d——'d" this day.

So arm in arm, we sought the Hall,
  Where onwards rolled the stream,
Through iron gate, with chain and ball,
  That kept incessant scream—
I jogg'd my friend, and said, is not
  This meant by wags a symbol ?
They've hung up here this cannon shot,
  To shew there's room to tremble,
      For war, this day.

He smiled and said, "pray, forward march,
  A truce with jibes and goads—
See, here's a great Collossal arch"—
  I ask'd if 't came from Rhodes ?
But when I heard it was a work,
  Built up for great Fayette,
Egad! said I, his foes at York
  Must hang their heads and fret,
      To see't this day.

Now on the spacious square we stood,
  My soul I felt expanding,
My eye pursued the dazzling flood
  Of James as he went winding;
I saw him raging far above,
  And with the rocks contending,
Then lower down, less furious move,
  As if his rage was spending
      Full fast, that day.

8*

Before me stood sweet Liberty!
　All light, and chaste, and airy,
Thy Temple tow'ring to the sky,
　Thy safe and lofty eyry!!
There—there it is, I inward thought,
　We nurse the infant Eagle,
And when to full grown strength he's brought;
　"Fell swoop" at things illegal,
　　　He'll make some day.

As right and left I turn my eye,
　Far flashing light assails,
From splendid domes that scatter'd lie
　Upon a thousand hills;
But dark as Erebus below,
　Black wreaths of smoke arise,
Where commerce follows James' flow
　Then pale, they fade in brighten'd skies,
　　　So sweet, this day.

What interchange of hill and dale!—
　It was indeed a lovely scene,
Of island—bridge, and silver sail,
　And scatter'd tree that waved between :
Nay, more—it had a touch sublime,
　For as I stood to scan,
My thoughts went back to former time,
　To thine, old Powhatan!
　　　So changed this day.

But time would fail to tell of *him*,
　I'll sing no dismal ditty,
I'll now pursue my idle whim,
　And dash my tear of pity—
One word, however, as we pass,
　Smith, had he laid his hands on
Smyth, Banks & Co. would not, alas,
　Have kill'd his great, great grandson
　　　So dead one day.

On ev'ry side, in glittering pride,
　Each lass herself was showing,
The bonnet wide, disdained to hide
　Her cheek with beauty glowing—

The brilliant silk—the dazzling shawl,
  The plumes that fell so wavy;
The jaunty air—the one and all
  Made me to cry peccavi!—
    I've sinn'd this day.

The bucks!—of them I took no notes,
  I hardly saw the wretches—
I guess they wore *straight jacket* coats,
  And *petticoats* for breeches—
They mar too much, man's form divine,
  But girls! somehow they get ye,
'Tis throwing pearls before the swine;
  My garters! how it frets me,
    To see 't some day.

While in my breast this envious thought
  Finds place and deeply rankles,
Up to the steps the crowd is brought,
  That place for showing *ankles*—
The heads of girls were in such whirls,
  Their tongues kept such a clinking,
They gave their curls some graceful twirls,
  But cared not, who was blinking
    At feet, that day.

The lofty flight of steps o'erpast,
  We gain'd at length the House,
With awe my mind was overcast,
  It made me still as mouse—
My friend, to whom I held me tight,
  Led through the grand Rotund,
And there I saw a reverend sight
  That nail'd me to the ground
    At once, that day.

In marble stillness!—calm!—sublime!—
  The Father of his country stands,
Serene majestic, as in time
  At head of his immortal bands—
In freedom's vestibule, he guards
  The passway to her Hall,
To point at once to great rewards
  And traitors' hearts appal
    With dread some day.

But who are these who chatter round,
  Their paltry wares here vending?—
Shall they profane this sacred ground?
  To h–ll let them be wending—
The money changers once were driven
  From God's own holy temple,
And here, as we have hopes o' Heaven,
  Let's take the great example
    Was set that day.

With thoughts of scorn, we hasten off,
  Press through the crowded lobby,
Before the lads of hawk and cough
  Had got upon their hobby—
The wish'd for land is now in view,
  We push across old Jordan,*
He foams and swells—it will not do,
  He's forced to yield, friend Gordon;
    He's dry this day.

A sorry sight now meets my eye,
  A plainer strikes on no man's,
They seem but men like you or I,
  I thought to see old Romans—
Here sit in rows a motley crew,
  Within a large quadrangle,
On seats alternate rais'd to view,
  That all who choose to wrangle
    May do't this day.

Upon the left, midway the Hall,
  You must not think I'm scoffin',
There stands a sort of what d'ye call,
  Just like a long black coffin—
'Tis rais'd somewhat above the floor,
  A table has, and standish;
'Twas built no doubt in days of yore,
  Ecod! It looks outlandish
    At this late day.

* Sergeant at arms.

They call it here the Speaker's seat,
  The Speaker he was in it—
And now and then, rose on his feet,
  But only for a minute ;
The thing's miscall'd as others are,
  Lucus a non Lucendo ;
He doth not *speak* so much, I'll swear,
  By half, as other men do,
      Who rise this day.

'Twould not be right—he must look grand,
  And bear himself full proudly—
His patience tax to understand
  What they are bleth'ring loudly—
Poor man ! I would not have his trade,
  For all its great attractions,
To list to each *"fanfaronade"*
  Of "nonsense and abstractions."

He has to sit and fix his eye,
  And bow, as comprehending—
But faith, at times he looks so sly,
  I think he's not attending—
A gape I've seen, in vain suppress'd,
  Convulse his handsome features,
And lurking smile has then confess'd,
  "Deuce take the prosing creatures.
      I'll doze some day."

Just at his feet, in cloth of green,
  There was a table standing,
And several men were round it seen,
  Who pen with ink were handling—
One rose, and with stentorian throat,
  Read out some clishma-claver—
Two others seem'd as taking note
  Of all they did palaver,
      Or read that day.

And now and then some man came out
  And strutted to the table,
I'm thinking what he was about,
  To tell, he'd not be able—

He'd seat himself with pompous air,
  And write so many letters,
Thinks I, my lad, you'd best take care,
  Such things have killed your betters,
    Before this day.

But what surprised me most of all,
  And what I thought improper,
Was constant motion 'bout the Hall
  And want of some mouth stopper—
And men whom we have proudly put
  In that august Assembly,
So cram their g–t with plum and nut,
  They must feel *"wooly wambly,"*
    I think some day.

Besides—there is another thing—
  When each should be attending,
They seem to give their fancy wing,
  And glances up are sending—
I think their necks must get a crick,
  As gall'ry-ward they're straining,
Such wicked thought, and boyish trick
  Grave men should be disdaining,
    On such a day.

But heavens! it is a lovely sight,
  My friends! I must excuse ye,
Those charming tints of red and white
  May well enough confuse ye—
How could ye turn to earth your eyes
  And look on man's coarse features,
When stars were glittering in the skies,
  And such transcendent creatures
    Were seen that day.

How would it do to pass a law,
  A Salic law in raillery,
By which t' enact that lasses braw
  Should not ascend the gallery?—
How many votes d'ye think 'twould get?
  Not one, I do protest—
But Pegasus, come, cease curvet,
  I think we've done our best
    To please this day.

I'll only add a postscript short,
  'Bout him they did elect—
And make a very brief report
  Of those they did reject—
The last must here be mention'd first—
  Two men of high renown ! !
Their glorious deeds were all rehears'd—
  Their like was never known
      Before this day.

One, "*firm as rocks*," was orthodox,
  The other 'd been to Spain—
But oh ! hard knocks of ballot box
  What hero can sustain ?
A father's deeds ! a country's debt,
  The spending all at Freedom's call !
A sun in glorious honor set,
  Were told, but disregarded all
      By some, that day.

I think that *one* had done much better,
  But for his warmest friends—
They read a Washingtonian letter,
  All letters ! seize ye fiends ! !—
This letter told of *blood and wounds*,
  Plots by the Federal gentry,
And how John Adams meant, by zounds,
  To bribe the Upper Country,
      With roads, some day.

A western man jump'd up in doubt,
  And asked to hear't again,
He caught a glimpse of cloven foot,
  And wish'd to see it plain—
Oh, do not take your specks, Smyth out,
  But prithee take a gag—
The cat has clearly turn'd about,
  And jump'd from out the bag,
      Quite plain, this day.

You've run your friend upon a ledge,
  He's dead *to-day* as Chelsea,
As dead as Smith could kill with sledge,
  As every one may *well see;*

"Oh that mine enemy would write
 A book," cried Job of old—
Translated wrong—we should indite,
 "*A letter,*" I will hold
  A bet, this day.

But here my muse her wing "*maun cower,*"
 Like Burns, in Tam O'Shanter;
They gave old warrior Giles the power,
 And off they all did canter—
His "*blushing honors*" *thickly* borne,
 No frost of age can wither;
They bloom as fresh as when full blown,
 And more he yet may gather,
  I hope, some day.

His body's worn by ruthless time,
 His head is now grown hoary,
But still his mind is in its prime,
 His sun will set in glory—
He's saved of late, our good old State,
 And pluck'd her honor drowning,
And when thus great, he yields to Fate,
 May angels there be crowning
  His head that day.

One word for what came after;
 I vow 'twas most amusing,
Some dying were with laughter,
 And some were heard abusing—
Some said it was a happy choice,
 And some "*the most infernal;*"
And some drawl'd out, in dol'rous voice,
 Good-by to things *internal*
  This blessed day.

Some got a squeeze, and some a jog,
 And fain would they have curst ye,
And some push'd on to get their grog,
 They were so dev'lish thirsty—
They had not ta'en a single drop
 For almost half an hour,
Such abstinence would break them up,
 'Twas far beyond their power
  To staud't each day.

The girls came tripping down the stairs,
  Midst rattling and thumping—
And each play'd off her pretty airs
  To set our hearts a jumping—
Fair Ladies all, I make my bow,
  And hope from bottom of my soul,
Tho' distance must divide us now,
  We'll find you at the Capitol,
    Some other day.

POETS AND POETRY.

Poetry's unnatural; no man ever talked in poetry 'cept a beadle on boxin' day, or Warren's blackin', or Rowland's oil, or some o' them low fellows. Never you let yourself down to talk poetry, my boy.—*Weller, senior.*

MR. EDITOR :—Although named after the wisest man that ever lived, I am afraid that you will think me very foolish to be troubling you with my complaints; yet seeing that my great namesake did not always the thing that was right, and moreover, that you did not despise my former communication, but put it down in black and white, I am tempted again to address you. I have given up travelling as I told you, but somehow or other, this world is so strangely constituted, that do as we will, there must be something to perplex and annoy us, and how to get rid of my present grievance I cannot divine. It is therefore that I fly to you in my distress, hoping that your superior wisdom may suggest some way of relief.

Almost all your contributors, I observe, stick up a kind of sign-board at the top of their writings, and you see I have followed their example; I think it a good custom. It answers a useful purpose, because your readers may be considered as a sort of travellers, who like to know which way they are going. Whether they be in search of business or pleasure, they can take the one road or the other; according to the sign, and by these useful contrivances, they can always know where to stop for "cakes and beer," or more solid fare. Let nobody stop with me, who cannot be satisfied with the humblest cheer.

When I tell you, Mr. Editor, that I am like the man who never made but one rhyme in his life, and that was "Thumpin and Dumpling," missing it then too, you may well wonder that poetry should be my theme; but I have been so much vexed and worried by poets, that I am almost as mad as Hogarth's "enraged musician;" and, if I may judge from the manner in which they have beset *you*, I have no doubt, if you could come out openly, you would wish the whole fraternity at the bottom of the sea; and I have a shrewd notion that you think with my Lord Byron, that if they have drunk of the true Castalian, *"it has a villainous twang."*

I have somewhere read of an old gentleman, who estimated his books according to their ponderousness. The folios were the best because they gave him the soundest naps; and, for my part, I never read poetry but for the purpose of going to sleep; for positively, I can hardly understand half of it. The words are so transposed for the sake of the rhyme, and the thoughts are so far-fetched, that it fatigues me to death to find out what the writer means. Blank verse especially, is to me, more incomprehensible than the demonstration we used to call at school—*Hot Hell*—and shall I confess it? Yes, and a thousand others would do the same, if they were as candid as I am. I never could get through the divine Milton in my life. As old Tom Mann Randolph once said, of his opponent in debate, "I cannot follow the gentleman; he is too erratic—he shakes hands with the comets." I never attempt to read Paradise Lost, without being convinced of my *fallen state,* when I awake, and find myself on the floor. Is there any conceivable subject, much less the devil and his imps, upon which human attention can be kept awake through twelve tedious books? If I could read by steam, I should feel as if I were dragging along twelve burthen cars. I have selected Milton to illustrate my feelings, because he is of unquestioned eminence; and if it be thus with me at the fountain head, what must I endure upon the tempest-tost ocean of modern poetry? By-the-by, blank verse! What is the meaning of the word blank? Like the fellow who had been writing prose all his life, without knowing it, here have I been reading blank verse all my life, without once inquiring into its meaning. I suppose I was satisfied from not comprehending it, that it was all a blank; but let us see what the dictionary says, for people now-a-days, I believe, are fed upon the dictionary. Blank—white, unwritten, confused, without rhyme; truly, an excellent definition! It is *confused* indeed, and Milton's verse is, to use his own words, "*confusion worse confounded.*" Can any sober man like you or I, Mr. Editor, read his account of Hell and the Devil, Sin and Death, Old Night and Chaos, without feeling his head a perfect chaos? What monstrous conceptions! What inconceivable descriptions! What unutterable horrors! Was the man mad? No wonder he was blind; for the bare imagination of such sights as he describes was enough to make any body blind. Indeed, it seems to me to be absolutely necessary to be blind, or at least to shut one's eyes, to imagine such a multitude of devils—more I dare swear than "vast hell can hold." Just shut your eyes for a moment, and observe the variety of objects you will see of all shapes and sizes. It must have been in this way that his imagination "*bodied forth the forms of things unknown.*" Some of his descriptions are really so ludicrous that one cannot forbear laughing outright; I am sure I cannot. For instance, Sin, in giving an account of her birth, says, that all at once Satan had the head-ache, and his head threw forth flames thick and fast, till the left side of it opened, and out she jumped—a goddess armed; what followed then, is too horrible for decent people to talk about. Again, when Moloch proposes to attack the Almighty with "*infernal thunder, and for lightning to shoot black fire and horror,*" among the angels, who can refrain from smiling at this new kind of ammunition. I should think *black fire* must be the least destructive sort. I know that I hate to see *my* fire look black of a cold day, and as for horror, where it was to be got and how used, I leave for devils to explain ; but enough of this nonsense. I did not set down to criticise Milton.—Heaven help me ! No, I am too conscious of the *longo intervallo* between him and a *thumping and dumplin* sort of fellow like myself; but I must take leave to say, that not one in a thousand of common folks, mind I say of common folks, who affect to be mightily pleased with Paradise Lost, can expound the following quotation :

> "They pass the planets seven, and pass the fix'd
> And that Crystalline sphere, whose balance weighs,
> The trepidation talk'd, and that first moved."

Can there be any pleasure in reading what requires so much labour to understand ? No, sir, it was not to criticise, but to beseech you to urge people, who cannot write poetry, to let it alone, and do as I did. I once took it into my head, that I could draw, and was always making the most uncouth things in the world, but still could not be convinced of my incapacity that way, until one day as I was sketching a head of the Marquis La Fayette, a friend peeped over my shoulder and asked me, if that was a water jug I was drawing. A water jug!! The head of La Fayette mistaken for a water jug!!! Mortified to death, I threw down my pencil, and secretly vowed that I was done with that business forever. Just so entreat those who never dipped their "jugs into the real Hippocrene," to break them at once, and pursue some more profitable calling. I know well that Dean Swift, or somebody, has said, that every one must have a poetical purging at some period of life; but he never intended that any one should bring on a diarrhœa of poetry. I have, sir, in my neighborhood, a run mad poet; and I ask you to recommend what can be done to restore the man to his senses. If Chalmers can cure a man of drunkenness, surely you might compound a dose which would cure my neighbor of his propensity to rhyme. I was in hopes that some of your versifiers had given him a dose that he never could get over, but he is at it again—and worse than ever. Ought he not to be sent to the lunatic hospital? For you know that a poet has himself said,

"The lunatic, the lover, and the poet,
Are of imagination all compact."

What am I doing? Plague on the fellow, he has absolutely infected me with his propensities—but let me describe him. He goes about with a sesquipedalian volume of poems, six inches thick, in a large side pocket; and there is no subject which can be introduced into conversation, that he is not immediately ready to draw out his heavy artillery and fire away upon you. He has made an acrostic upon every man, woman, and child in the county; and I'll tell you how he does it; he says it is the simplest thing in the world. He writes down the initials and then without any manner of reference to the particular individual to be described, he writes whatever enters his head, and is as well satisfied with his productions, as if they were the finest portraits. I could cut out as good verse with a broad-axe. He is besides, a perfect poetical Jackdaw, and is so tricked out in other people's feathers, that you dare not open your mouth, but he is ready for you with quotations innumerable. He beats Dr. Pangloss hollow. This is sufficiently annoying, but nothing to the inflictions of his own rhymes. Not a cat nor a dog can die, but he writes an epitaph. Marriage with us is absolutely discouraged—because the young people are afraid of an epithalamium. It is dangerous to admit him into your house, for he goes away and describes every mother's son of you. He has caused some of my most valuable acquaintances to emigrate to the western country. In short he keeps a *Poetical Bank and discounts paper. Our whole community is flooded with his notes.* There is no danger of *his* stopping. I wish there was. He is truly a dreadful animal, and ought to be treated, as the ancients did their mischievous bulls. He should have hay upon his head;—*Fœnum habet cornu,* ought to be graven on his forehead. His effrontery is the most unblushing. He reads his own productions without shame, and looks around with an air of triumph for approbation. He declares he was born a poet, and cannot help writing if he would; that he has the divine afflatus, and must pour out his abundant thoughts. He takes snuff to excess, and says he has a most *hexcellent foice*. Now, sir, can you imagine a greater bore? Even sleep, my favorite resort, is denied me; for he will not suffer me to sleep, but like a fly, is perpetually tickling my nose with "how do you like that?" "mark this," and "observe that." I groan in spirit, but the fellow has no bowels of compassion. Sometimes in a frenzy I jump up and rush out, but he follows me, and continues reading long after I get out of the reach of his *foice*. With all this, he has not the most distant idea of his own absurdity. Once I slept in the same room with him; I say slept, because by great good luck his poetical blunderbuss had been left down stairs. In the middle of the night, I felt some one shaking me; and opening my eyes, there he stood over me, in his shirt-t—l, with a candle in one hand, and a written paper in the other, to read to me some beautiful thoughts which he had been embodying. He has written a sort of mock heroicomical poem, which it was my purpose to send you with my annotations and reflections. It is called the Diviad, and is founded upon a story which was current some years ago, of one of our Pres——ts, who was remarkably fond of swimming, and who, upon one occasion, went out with his son to the Potomac, and in the course of their aquatic pranks overturned their boat, and lost all their clothes. After various attempts to recover them by diving, they succeeded in obtaining a portion of the habiliments of the father and son, but not enough to rig out the former for a becoming entrance into Washington. By sending off the son, a cabinet council was called, consisting of B——, S——, C——, and R——, who respectively gave their opinions to his majesty mounted upon his throne (viz. the bottom of the boat,) as to the most advisable mode of getting back to Washington without an exhibition of his nudity; but I must stop, or I shall tire you as much as he has tired me. I know that this is *"rayther* a *sudden pull up,"* as Mr. Weller says; but the art of writing, according to Sam, is to make the reader *vish there vos more.*

Very respectfully,

Your most obd't, humble servant,

SOLOMON SOBERSIDES.

~~~~~~~~~~~~~~

JOHN ADAMS' SON, MY JO, JOHN.

John Adams' Son, my Jo, John, when we were first
  acquent,
I did na dream your aim was, to be the President;
Ye've got unto the tap, John, but have an eye below,
Ye're ganging down as fast as up, John Adams' Son,
  my Jo.

John Adams' Son, my Jo, John, when Party here began
To raise her horrid head, John, ye were a Fed'ral man,
And ye, amang us a', John, did hate the Demoes so,
We thought ye then a trusty frien', John Adams' Son,
  my Jo.

John Adams' Son, my Jo, John, what pleasure did it gie
In Alien and Sedition days to see ye gang wi' me?
Ah! *"palsied"* be the Press, John, it teased your Fa-
  ther so;
We did our best to stap its breath, John Adams' Son,
  my Jo.

John Adams' Son, my Jo, John, it blew us all *"sky
  high,"*
And may be brought *"a drap,"* Sir, a drap intil your
  "eye,"
But soon there came a time, John, the lucky Em—
  bar—go,
And then ye took a tack about, John Adams' Son, my Jo.

John Adams' Son, my Jo, John, we wanted then nae
  "light,"
"Great Jefferson had said ye must," and surely he was
  right,
So on ye drave the scheme, John, it was a maister blow,
And sent ye to St. Petersburg, John Adams' Son, my Jo.

John Adams' Son, my Jo, John, we thought ye turned
 aside,
And did na see what was the trick, *"the ass in lion's
 hide,"*
But late ye've bray'd so loud, John, we ken ye now,
 oh ho!
How *"stupid"* we!—*"ineffably!"*—John Adams' Son,
 my Jo.

John Adams' Son, my Jo, John, ye must be deep at play,
Or must have got the help, mon, of Maister Speaker
 Clay;
But how came ye to bray, John, so soon, I want to know,
Ye'll sure be beat by Jacky's Son, John Adams' Son,
 my Jo.

John Adams' Son, my Jo, John, ye've brought about
 your fa'
By saying *ye wad* send men to Isthmus Pan—a—ma;
And then to cap the climax, John, John Sergeant he
 must go—
That chiel who wants the Blackies free, John Adams'
 Son, my Jo.

John Adams' Son, my Jo, John, what said old Wash-
 ing—ton?
"Trade, trade wi' ev'ry nation—get tangled up wi' none."
Tak' back the silly pledge, the pledge of Jim Monroe,
Or say it was *"a pledge to self,"* John Adams' Son,
 my Jo.

John Adams' Son, my Jo, John, why go to Pan–a–ma?
What profit under heaven, can we be getting there?
How can ye think to change, John, the laws o' na-
 tions so,
Or Catholics to Protestants, John Adams' Son, my Jo.

John Adams' Son, my Jo, John, let Hayti, mon, alone,
Things hae been fixed wi' her sure, this mony a year
 agone;
We want no *consuls black*, John, to rouse domestic foe,
Guid folks enou' at work for that, John Adams' Son,
 my Jo.

John Adams' Son, my Jo, John, 'twould be a maister
    stroke,
Gin ye could put to death soon, that fellow *Roanoke;*
Ye've tried to prove him mad, John, but oh, it will na do,
He is na mad nor Tazwell fou, John Adams' Son, my Jo.

John Adams' Son, my Jo, John, ye've climb'd the
    highest steeple,
But dinna tak it in your head to scorn the Sov'reign
    People;
Ye're getting Ultra Fed', John, and lift too high your
    pow,
Draw in that cloven foot, ye de'il, John Adams' Son,
    my Jo.

John Adams' Son, my Jo, John, turn down to earth
    your eyes,
And dinna talk o' building *"Light Houses o' the Skies;"*
Quit *"Exploration"* schemes, John, and ilka thing
    forego,
They ca' *unconstitutional,* John Adams' Son, my Jo.

THE VICAR OF BRAY.

In my good Father's royal days,
  The reign nick-nam'd of terror;
    A zealous Monarchist I was,
  And never own'd my error—
    All Democrats were Jacobines,
  Agog for Revolution;
    And "Rights of Man" were but the means
  To kick up some confusion,
    And this is true I will maintain,
  And so will Hen y Cl y, sir.
    That ev'ry man who wants to reign,
  Must be a Vicar of Bray, sir.

When Jefferson obtained the throne,
  I felt a deep conviction:
    In Congress Hall I made it known,
  And voted for Restriction—

The Terrapin was then the thing,
Most worthy imitation,
  And not such geese as Pickering;
So down with Exportation:
      And this is true I will maintain,
      And so will Hen y Cl y, sir;
        That ev'ry man who wants to reign,
        Must be a Vicar of Bray, sir.

When Madison eclips'd Monroe,
I did my service tender,
  And soon was sent a Plenipo,
To Russian Alexander—
  The loaves and fishes thus I got,
And gull'd th' Administration,
  Nor did I care a single groat,
For former friend's damnation:
      And this is true I will maintain,
      And so will Hen y Cl y, sir;
        That ev'ry man who wants to reign,
        Must be a Vicar of Bray, sir.

When James the Second proved to be,
"The star of the ascendant,"
  I plotted my catastrophe,
As I was still dependent—
  And so you see it came to pass
In Fortune's wild vagary,
  "Write poor Dogberry down an ass,"
But write me Secretary:
      And this is true I will maintain,
      And so will Hen y Cl y, sir;
        That ev'ry man who wants to reign,
        Must be a Vicar of Bray, sir.

Great Britain once I did adore,
But now I took my cue, sir;
  Her greatness, pshaw! twas all a bore,
And I began t' abuse her—
  I kept a sharp lookout ahead,
Ran down the English nation,
  As all who wish may fully read
In my July oration:

And this is true I will maintain,
And so will Hen y Cl y, sir;
 That ev'ry man who wants to reign,
Must be a Vicar of Bray, sir.

When Jemmy's eight long years were gone,
I'm free to be confessor,
 I fix'd my eye upon the throne,
For who could tell successor?
 But when I heard the People roar,
And saw their clear intent, sir,
 I play'd old Talleyrand once more
And wooed the man of Ghent, sir:
  And this is true I will maintain,
  And so will Hen y Cl y, sir;
   That ev'ry man who wants to reign,
  Must be a Vicar of Bray, sir.

So Hal and I were cup and can,
He Congress-men could twist, sir,
 And triumph'd o'er the great Hang-man,
T' Arbuthnot and Ambrister!
 We boldly argued *him* unfit,
To fill such lofty stations.
 Who I myself before had writ
Was right by laws o' nations:
  And this is true I will maintain,
  And so will Hen y Cl y, sir;
   That ev'ry man who wants to reign
  Must be a Vicar of Bray, sir.

Th' illustrious Coalition, and
"Safe precedent succession,"
 For these I'll join both heart and hand,
"While I can keep possession ;"
 And by my plighted faith, dear Clay,
With you I will not palter,
 And you shall have my place one day,
"Unless my mind should alter:"
  And this is true I will maintain,
  And so will Hen y Cl y, sir;
   That ev'ry man who wants to reign
  Must be a Vicar of Bray, sir,

And now I'm firmly seated high,
I may have some opinion,
  I need no longer now deny
I hate the Old Dominion—
  Her stubborn pride must now succumb,
Her strength he lost by fractures,
  We've got her down beneath our thumb,
By dint of manufactures:
      And this is true I will maintain
    And so will Hen y Cl y, sir;
      That ev'ry man who wants to reign
    Must be a Vicar of Bray, sir,

No longer palsied will we sit,
But with one mighty movement,
  We'll ruin our Constituents yet,
By means of their *improvement*—
  We'll make a splendid kingdom rise
Like European nations.
  And from Light Houses of the Skies,
We'll send them Corruscations:
      And this is true I will maintain
    And so will Hen y Cl y, sir;
      That ev'ry man who wants to reign
    Must be a vicar of Bray, sir.

~~~~~~~~~~~~~~~

TO TOBACCO.

Food fills the wame an' keeps us livin'
Tho' life's a gift no worth receivin,'
When heavy dragg'd wi' pine an' grievin'
    But oil'd by thee,
  The wheels o' life gae downhill, screivin;
    Wi' rattlin glee.—*Burns.*

Some talk of black eyed girls and blue,
And some of cheeks of rosy hue,
Of wit and wine and friendship true;
    They're well enough—
Tobacco!! give me thee to chew
    To smoke, or snuff.

Oh! fragaant plant where'er you are,
In box or pouch, or sweet segar,
Havanna! Brown's! or Maccabau!
    Thou best of weeds!
Crown him the first of Bards, by far,
    Who sings thy deeds.

I love to sit and see thee curl'd
In circling smoke, and upward whirl'd,
A pinch of snuff for all the world!
    At such a time—
Unto the winds my cares be hurl'd:
    I feel sublime,

When thou dost titilate my nose,
It seems to dissipate my woes,
I feel a thrill down to my toes
    Quite 'cap a pee,'
Ah! wretched he who never knows
    Thy joys, Rappee!

When cold compelleth us to wheeze
Who would exchange one glorious sneeze
For all the charms of all the shes
    For wealth or wine?
And what so soon can raise a breeze
    As Number Nine?

He who'd of ev'ry ill be rid,
Has but to take a monstrous quid
Into the mouth, let it be slid
    And draw the breath—
Then, like the reckless Richard Fid,
    Who cares for death?—

There's scarce a man in all this nation,
Of high or lowly occupation,
No matter what may be his station
    On life's long docket
But keeps you in some sort of fashion
    Snug in his pocket.

Your Tradesman with his hardy fist,
In ecstasy will grasp his twist

10

Within his cheek, thick as his wrist,
  He stows a whopper,
Just as the Miller chucks his grist
  Into his hopper.

Your Ploughman takes a thundering *chaw,*
And tucks it in distended jaw,
Then roars he out his *gee* and *haw,*
  So charm'd with you,
His very cattle seem to draw
  As if they knew.

The Tars who o'er the ocean sail,
Whose hearts in danger never quail,
What nerves them so to breast the gale
  And kiss the moon!
'Tis juice of thee, adored Pigtail!
  Thou greatest boon!

The Doctor warns us 'gainst a quid
If from diseases we'd be freed—
Then gravely opes his box's lid,
  And takes a chew,
The patient does as Doctor did,
  Though death ensue.

The Merchant takes much wiser views,
And ponders deeper o'er the news,
The *"cud of fancy"* sweeter chews
  While mumbling thee,
And better takes his mental cruise
  O'er tumbling sea.

The Lawyer turning o'er thy leaf
Can better comprehend his brief,
His cause set forth in bold relief
  With stronger power;
His fancy loves, 'tis my belief
  Thy *golden* shower.

I'll risk a bet e'en Johnny Q—
Has got a *"bargain"* oft in you;
And Clay, who knows a thing or two
  Is *"up to snuff,"*
And he who all the British slew
  Enjoys a puff.

Oh Burns! thou eulogist of whiskey
Which often made thee much too brisk, eh!
In drinking it, how greatly risk we;
    It plays the deuce,
Not so, let's say it, *Unusquisque*
    With this sweet juice.

Tobacco brings no man to ruin,
For very little serves for chewing,
And then he knows what he is doing,
    But as for whiskey
Some mischief 'tis forever brewing
    We feel so frisky.

Tobacco never plays us pranks
Nor throws poor bodies off their shanks,
Just reeling round as they were hanks
    In swift rotations,
While whiskey will upset all ranks,
    Through deep potations.

Then let Tobacco's fame be sung,
Oh may it roll o'er many a tongue
With it let every nose be wrung,
    Save women's noses;
For should they use it—old or young
    Love straightway dozes.

(For the Richmond Whig.)

MEETING OF THE LADIES AT THE CAPITOL.

"Aristocracy alone could ever have imagined it (community)
to mean a privileged class, and *sophistry* only would pretend to
include in it the women."

    Were I a Man
    I would remove these tedious stumbling blocks,
    And smooth my way upon their headless necks,
    And being a woman, I will not be slack
    To play my part in fortune's pageant.—*Hen. VI.*

Most lovely, accomplish'd, and ill treated Ladies!
Best part of creation!—attend to what said is—
Four Spinsters have met and determined together,
To call on the women, that is, if the weather

Be not too inclement to meet in the houses,
Where lately our Fathers, and Brothers, and *Spouses*
Have dared to proclaim to a thunder-struck nation,
That Ladies *have nothing to do in creation.*
'Tis known to mankind how we hate all contention,
But garters! and stars! we must go to Convention:
We call on the married—maids—widows and all,
From the Miss in her teens to the Miss with her doll,
To come in a body, and dress'd in their finest,
And try in their beauty, who'll look the divinest;
You may be assured that a thousand beholders
Will be there, of the men, both the non and freeholders
To gaze on the charms which may thus be collected,
To ask at their hands, that our rights be protected.
Girls! put on your bonnets, the biggest you wear,
Oh lud! we shall cover the Capitol Square;
There'll hardly be room for such monstrous umbrellas,
But gracious! these bonnets so please the young fellows;
The matrons can wrap themselves up in pelisses,
The blood must be warm'd as it gradually freezes.
Let every dear tabby, inclining to pur,
Put on her angolas and muffle in fur;
But we that are young must be splendid and flashing;
Our shawls must be worn in a manner quite dashing,
Half off the shoulder and carelessly winding,
As if they were trifles not worth our minding;
Ev'ry curl must be held in complete requisition,
Our object you see is to improve our condition;
Ev'ry lip that is red—ev'ry cheek that is rosy—
From the brightest of eyes to the eye that is dozy,
Must be sure to be ready to work on the souls
Who wish to exclude our sex from their *polls;*
Bring together in short ev'ry species of beauty,
"Virginia expects you will All do your duty."

We call on you, Daughters of old mother Eve!
To rise in your charms, and your rights to retrieve—
Nature never on earth, could have made such a blunder
As this, that the women be always kept under;
When ev'ry thing else in the world that is light
Gets up to the top, will you tell us 'tis right

That we tamely submit, in despite of her rules,
To be number'd with idiots, and class'd with the fools?—
Shall you who have dandled the brats on your knees,
And in Primers have taught 'em their A B and C's;
Who, Philosophers hold, have an infinite weight
In moulding their minds, be excluded from State?
Forbid it kind heaven!—these impudent frights
Have *diddled* themselves, by their own Bill of Rights.
"By nature all men are born equally free,"
But *men* are not *women!*—oh fiddle de dee !—
We say, and we deem it a great condescension,
We say, we will certainly go to Convention;
We'll send *ninety-six* of our prettiest girls,
And put all your noddles at once into whirls;
Your grave looking bodies—your Patricepaters
With ogles and sighs we could make 'em all traitors;
We wonder what monster would dare be so rude,
Such a bevy of beauty, from it to exclude?
We fear not the issue, we'll enter, and vote,
The Government change—Hurra! Petticoat!
Yes, that be the name! and in future all Writs
Shall run *"In the name of the Petticoat,"* chits!
We'll punish you well for your want of respect,
How *funny* you'll look when your heads are all peck'd!
Why should not the women be suffered to vote?
Is there any good reason, we beg you to show't—
Do you urge they are volatile, fickle, and frisky?
Not half so much so as the swillers of whiskey;
Are they ruled by their Fathers and Husbands with
    switches?
Nine-tenths we can tell you have put on the breeches;
Don't many pay taxes, and some of them fight?
A'nt you willing to do all that men do, Miss Wright?
They have governed as well as the men have, we guess,
What Monarch was wiser than English Queen Bess?
Go read of their chivalrous actions, and mark
What Hero did better than Joan of Arc?
Look at Cath'rine the great, and forbear, sirs, to scoff—
Poh! hush about Orloff—Potemkin—Zuboff—
We *all* have our follies, and none had 'em more
Than Henry the Fourth, whom you almost adore,
10*

Cleopatra—Zenobia—Semiramis Great!
E'en Pericles' mistress once govern'd the State :—
Examine, we pray, the Republic of letters,
And say if you can that the men are our betters;
What think you, ye poor and contemptible ninnies,
Of charming epistles like Madame Sevigne?
Of Genlis—of Dacier—of Madame de Stael?
They rush on the mind just as fast as the hail ;
What think you of Hamilton, Edgeworth, and Moore,
Of Opie and Hemans?—I'd count up a score—
Is it fit ?—is it right that such exquisite tongues
Should be mute, while your boobies are splitting their
      lungs.

We've thrown out a few of these hasty remarks,
Just to call your attention to some of our sparks—
Should they obstinate prove, should they turn us all out,
We are likely to have a most thundering rout ;
We don't care a pin—we are used to a squeeze,
Let's have an Assembly and issue decrees ;
Let us only be firm, and we venture our lives
They'll soon come among us to look for some wives ;
Yes—now is our time—we may do what we please,
We'll soon have the rebels all down on their knees,
And then !—oh the thought is too vast for the brains—
We'll make on the Treas'ry such terrible drains—
We'll sparkle in jewels—we'll have such a ball! !—
And—what shall we have ?—come, come to the Hall.

FOUR SPINSTERS.

[For the Richmond Whig.]

A RECEIPT

FOR MAKING A LONG SPEECH UPON ANY GIVEN SUBJECT.

Promising is the very air o' the time: it opens the eyes of ex-
pectation: Performance is ever the duller for his act; and but in
the plainer and simpler kind of people, the deed of saying is quite
out of use.— *Timon of Athens, Act V.*

You must gracefully rise, with a bow, from your chair,
And begin—Mister Speaker!—with dignified air,

You had not intended to utter *one word,*
Where too much already, perhaps, has been heard;
But yet, notwithstanding, you find that you *must,*
Or you would not discharge, as you should do, your
    trust;
You have not a hope you can shed a new ray
Where suns have been shining so brightly all day;
You will not attempt it—you are not so silly,
As soon *"gild the gold,"* and as well *"paint the lily;"*
But you *must* be indulged, for a very short while,
Though your language be homely, and homely your
    style;
It is far from your purpose to make a long speech,
You must scrape on your fiddle, although it should
    screech.
Yes, promise the House, you will be very brief,
Just tell 'em so, man,—it will be a relief—
Protest that in all which you now mean to say,
You mean to be govern'd by strict cour—te—sy;
No member must think it—oh never—no, no,
That you mean to be cruel, and tread on his toe;
'Tis not your intention to break through the rules,
Nor hint that all men but yourself are turn'd fools;
Each man has a right to maintain his opinion,
Long as Freedom shall reign in this Ancient Dominion;
You mean not to breathe a suspicion—'od's life!!
No doubt they are chaste as was Cæsar*—his wife.
Having taken this dazzling and beautiful flight,
Your exordium is free, sir, from ev'ry thing trite.

Go on now, with all that you do not intend,
And this is a subject almost without end.
Be sure, notwithstanding, in doing the same,
That you say ev'ry thing you pretend to disclaim;
Then mention the field which you mean to explore,
Though you never should think of your promises more.
Go back to the days of old Adam and Eve,
With the world in a sling, you may laugh in your sleeve;

---

* The nature of this compliment seems somewhat equivocal, Cæsar himself being the greatest gallant in all Rome.—*Vide Plutarch in vit. Cæs.*

Fight over the *"duel"* of Cain and of Abel,*
Produce the confusion of Tower of Babel;
Let nothing deter you—but at 'em again,—
Some *brass* you may borrow from one Tubal-cain;†
Throw in, by the way of a passing remark,
The form and dimensions of old Noah's Ark;
Surveying the Flood, you may then talk of Moses;
All this, you observe, your *research,* man, exposes;
Go down, Sir, to Egypt—set th' Israelites free,
And smother King Pharaoh and all in the sea;
Cephrænes and Cheops!—tell all that they did,
And settle the doubt of the great Py—ra—mid.
Pshaw! pay no attention to *nodding* and *winks,*
But mention the sands which half buried the Sphinx;
Be sure you remember the siege of old Troy,
Not many have heard of that business, my boy;
I'd give *a tenth part of an ephah—an omer,*‡
To see their eyes shut like the eyes of poor Homer;
The great Trojan horse will be excellent now,
With *"a wreath of abstractions"* encircling "his brow;"
"Virginia must ride him"—some fellows rakehelly
"Must jump with stilettoes § *all sharp from his belly;"*
Timeo Danaos et dona ferentes
Will come in so pat—the quotation quite spent is;
But do not omit it on any account, sir—
Let Pegasus blow now—and then I'll remount, sir.

So, Pegasus—now for a different gait,
You've jolted me on at a terrible rate—
Sir!—glance at the tale of the Golden Fleece,
And give 'em the whole of Gillies' his Greece.

* In the debate on the duelling question, a distinguished orator contended that the first *duel* upon record was that between Cain and Abel.

† And Zillah, she also bare Tubal-cain, an instructor of every artificer in brass —*Genesis.*

‡ Now an Omer is the tenth part of an Ephah.—10 *chap. Exodus, v.* 36.

§ According to the best commentators upon the Iliad, stilettoes were hardly in use at the siege of Troy, but the word must stand —it is so in the roll.—*See Debate on Convention.*

The customs of Sparta, proceed to discuss,
And make 'em a drink of the "*Nigrum jus;*"*
Ask if among them the bravest man
Would'nt glory to think of the "epitan."†
Lycurgus of course bring in—because
Few ever heard of Lycurgus his laws;
Athens in order you'll add to these
And all the heroes that end in "es."
Bring in the man with the oyster shell,
Who hated, but why—he could not tell;
Tell 'em old Socrates' head was bald,
Xantippe, his wife, a horrible scold;
That his nose was flat, and the poor old cock
Made away with himself with accurs'd hemlock;
What a pity he could'nt have worn a wig,‡
Before he was driven to this last swig—
That the laws of Draco were written in blood,
But Solon's laws were uncommonly good;
That Plato's republic was theoretic,
And Aristotle a peripatetic;
That Diogenes lived in a sort of a tub,
And gave somebody a cynical rub.
Having gone thus far, you may throw in happily,
A sketch of the battle of old Thermopylæ;
Then after a dash of war and slaughter,
You'll ask for a tumbler glass of water—
Having *scoured up Greece,* go over to Rome,
And there you will find nobody at home.
Remus and Romulus suck'd a she wolf,
And Curtius, the blockhead, jump'd into a gulf;

* *Nigrum jus,* I address myself to the unlearned, was neither more nor less than *Black Broth,* a Spartan drink which the loudest advocate for reform would scarcely be prevailed upon to substitute for brandy, although we are now in a state of nature as they contend, and are referred to Sparta as the model of our new constitution.

† He tan epi tan. The glorious declaration of the Spartan ladies, which I will leave the beaux to translate to ours.

‡ This exclamation seems quite natural when we behold the many transformations from age to youth by this most ingenious contrivance—qui capit ille facit, not the wig.

A King cut a grindstone in two with a razor,
Cheer'd on by an *Augur*, who stood by a gazer ;
Porsenna came there, with a murderous band,
And a fool, they call'd Scævola, burnt off his hand.
The kingdom—republic—agrarian laws,
Press all of them into your glorious cause ;
Sip more of the water—not porter—oh Tims,
And tell 'em the tale of the belly and limbs ;
Show 'em the Capitol, rescued by *geese*,
And ask if the like will e'er happen in this ;
The Tarpeian rock, and the overturn'd Gauls,
Compare them to Shockoe—and warn 'em of squalls ;
But time, sir, would fail me to go over grounds,
Where Pompey and Cæsar and other blood-hounds
Gave lessons to millions, who after should live,
That power's a thing 'tis imprudent to give ;
So in short, that they lose not a word of it all,
Just read 'em Ned Gibbon's Declension and Fall.
By this they're impatient to moisten their throats,
And now is your time to *unkennel* your *notes ;*
Exhibit your papers—unfold your *foolscap,*
In place of their dinner, they'll all take a nap.
Now fancy yourself in a cyphering School,*
That nincompoop Cocker to you is a fool ;
Come show 'em as plain as that men are alive,
That *"five is a hondre,"* and *"hondre is five ;"*†
Demonstrate by pounds, by shillings and pence,
'Tis *nonsense* to listen to old *common sense ;*
And tell 'em—yes, tell 'em—amaze the beholder,
The man who pays taxes, is not the Freeholder ! ! ! !

Oh rattle away and *"bother their gigs,"*
No matter how much they may sigh for their swigs ;
Then take in extenso, the statutes at large,
A volley of laws at the numskulls discharge,
And if they don't lustily halloo *"enough,"*
"Lay on" 'em, I beg you, "lay on" 'em,

MACDUFF.

---

* See debate on Convention, passim.
† This line is founded on fact—a Frenchman, many years ago,
offered to prove it by Algebra.

TO DYSPEPSIA.

Dyspepsia! horrid fiend, away!
Nor dog my steps from day to day:
  Where'er I go—wherever fly,
  I meet that dim and sunken eye.
That pallid and cadav'rous hue,
Those bloodless lips, so coldly blue,
  Thy tott'ring gait, and falt'ring breath
  Proclaim thee, messenger of death.

Behold thy work—my languid frame
Its vigor wasted, blood grown tame,
  Afraid of what, it cannot tell,
  Is held in thy demoniac spell;
Dark shadows round, thou seem'st to fling;
"My ears with hollow murmurs ring;"
  My head grows giddy—eyesight dim,
  My senses seem to reel and swim.

At night I start from hideous dream;
My pillow fly, with stifled scream;
  I dare not sleep—at early morn
  I hear the huntsman's echoing horn;
My burthened heart one instant bounds
To spring to horse, and cheer the hounds—
  Alas! no more for me the chase!
  Myself pursued, I fly thy face.

I cannot breathe the balmy air—
It cheers me not for thou art there;
  I am not gladden'd by the sun—
  His course is glorious, mine is run.
For me the flowers all vainly bloom,
They seem but things which strew the tomb
  All things that others seek, I shun—
  The earth a blank—the world undone.

Is there no power, this brow to cool,
And wash me in Siloam's pool?
  Bethesda's waters! where are they?
  The friendly hand to guide the way?

Remorseless fiend! relax thy hold;
The demons were cast out of old,
   And I will cling to Jesus' knee;
   Oh! let him speak, and thou must flee.

THE DELEGATE'S SOLILOQUY.

T' adjourn or not adjourn, that is the question:
Whether 'tis better for one here to suffer
The toils and labors of amassing money,
Or to stand firm against a sea of *motions*,
And by opposing, end them?—T' adjourn,—go home—
No more; and by adjournment, say we end
The heartache and the thousand natural shocks
That flesh is heir to.—'Tis a consummation
Devoutly to be wish'd. T' adjourn; go home;—
Go home! perchance *turn'd out!* aye, there's the rub;
For in that phrase, *go home,* what things are couch'd,
When we have shuffled off this *legal coil,*
Must give us pause: There's the respect
That makes our *sessions* of so long a life;
For who could bear these "fly-slow" hours of time;
Th' Alligator's* wrongs—the rich man's contumely,
The pangs of parted love—the *laws delay'd,*
The *log-rolling* for office—and the scoffs
That want of merit on a speaker brings,
When we ourselves might our quietus make
By a bare voting?—who would dullness bear
To chase and groan under a weary life,
But that the dread of something at one's home;
The ever wav'ring country, from whose bourne,
Few delegates return—puzzles the will
And makes us rather bear those ills we have
Than fly to greater, that we *know well* of—
Thus *interest* doth make cowards of us all,
And thus the native hue of good intention

* Assemblyman so called.

Is sickled o'er with the pale cast of *fear*,
And enterprizes of *no pith* or moment
With this regard, attentive ear receive
And *get* the name of action.

~~~~~~~~~~~~~~~~~~~~~

THE MAN IN THE MOON.

Yon lonely man, I've heard them say,
   Who looks from out the moon,
Broke, when on earth, the Sabbath day,
   And work'd—a worthless loon!—

When I first heard he was a man,
   It used to be my whim,
On lonely nights, his form to scan,
   Until my eyes grew dim.

Methought I saw, quite plain enough,
   His body, legs, and axe—
But then his head seem'd always off,
   Which made me doubt the facts.

A beacon in the sky, he stands,
   To warn poor sinful man
To rest that day, as God commands,
   And then to work again.

How cold he looks within the Moon!
   His shoulder'd axe he shows
And woodman like, with clouted shoon,
   He seems to wade through snows.

In winter, when the Moon doth swim
   Adown the clear cold sky,
And not a soul is out but him,
   There is he, still on high!

When storms deform her silv'ry face,
   Which now and then she shrouds,
There is he, ever in his place,
   Careering 'mid the clouds!

What art thou doing, lonely thing!
   With axe in that cold clime?
No wood thou'st e'er been seen to bring,
   In all recorded time.

There art thou left, a monument
   Of what on earth befel,
Still bent upon your vain intent,
   Like Sysiphus in hell.

So here on earth, fixed on a rock
   Out in the distant sea,
A scoffer* too was made a mock,
   As scoffers ought to be.

Your fate and his seem parallel,
   At least in some degree;
Your bosoms both became the hell,
   From which you could not flee.

But yet his fate was worse than yours,
   He only saw the sea
That wash'd far off the happy shores
   Where fondly he would be.

A wat'ry waste his prospect lone,
   Instead of glittering arms,
Which won for him a glorious throne—
   Naught else for him had charms.

Whilst thou, in thy resplendent car,
   Hast seen in its careers
All heaven, earth, and sea, and air,
   For many thousand years.

Let not thy wretched bosom pine,
   For such a world as this,
Methinks a punishment like thine
   Must have some smack of bliss.

But no—a sombre shade it flings,
   To feel guilt's constant goad,
And sea, earth, air, and heav'nly things,
   But aggravate the load.

* Napoleon.

Farewell to thee, old Anchorite—
And do not yet despair—
We'll come to you some lovely night
By sailing through the air.

Since you have left the earth for moon,
Man every thing can do,
And he, perchance, in silk balloon,
May come and chat with you.

MILITARY GLORY.

The bones of the soldiers who fell at Waterloo, have been dug up and transported to Hull in England, to be ground into manure and sold to the farmers.—*English Paper.*

Alas! what a picture is here,
And what shadows we vainly pursue!
Ye lovers of Glory! come near—
Lo, the field where in triumph the British flag flew!
The great Aceldama! the far-fam'd Waterloo!

Behold what of Glory survives!—
Here are wretches, exhuming the bones
Of heroes, who peril'd their lives,
And who fell amidst carnage, commingling their groans,
That the scourgers of earth might be seated on thrones.

To England they bear them to grind
Unto powder to fertilize land—
To her who hath borne them, consign'd;
And the dust of the son who died wielding his brand,
To be scatter'd on earth by a parent's own hand!!

Ambition! sit then on this plain,
Like the prophet Ezekiel of yore,
"Dry bones" are here *"shaking"* again—
"Will the flesh and the sinews come on them once more?"
"Or the breath come again, when they hear the winds
*roar?"**

* Ezekiel, chap. xxxvii.

Ah, yes, when the trumpet shall sound,
At whose summons the boldest heart faints!
But will they with laurels be crown'd?
No—the glory no tarnish from earth ever taints
Shall be theirs—*"The great army of martyrs and saints."*

The soldiers of Christ shall be crown'd,
When the trumpet shall rouse them from sleep;
Where then will earth's heroes be found?—
O'er this field and the fallen what heart but must weep?
For *"who soweth the wind, he the whirlwind must reap."**

PICTURES BY THE SUN.

I've studied thee, bright Sun, in many a lecture,
And at thy power have been filled with wonder;
But never dreamt that thou could'st make a picture,
Without the least defect, or smallest blunder;
Oh for a sight of those soft pictured pages
Thou hast *"Daguerreotyped"* for countless ages!

Of these, thou must have doubtless many legions,
As well of *this* world as of those far hence;
"Of Planets, Suns, and Adamantine regions,
Wheeling, unshaken, through the void immense;"†
Where hang those pictures?—in what mighty Louvre?
And which, I pray thee, was thy great *chef d'œuvre?*

When first thou look'dst upon the world then void—
When all was dark, and things about were bandied—
In taking sketches, wert thou then employ'd,
As ev'ry object into form expanded?
If so, and we could make thee, Sun, obey us,
We'd have that scene august, of *Ancient Chaos.*

We'd like to see our great first parent, Adam,
As when he strolled about his charming garden;
And as he gazed upon the first fair madam,
Who came to soften, but alas! did harden.

* Hosea, chap. viii.

† Planets, Suns, and Adamantine spheres
 Wheeling, unshaken, through the void immense.—*Akenside.*

Give us old Noah and his sons and daughters,
Just as they sailed upon the world of waters.

We fain would see too, if we now were able,
   The plain of Shinar, whence "men's sons" were driven
From that vast structure called the Tower of Babel,
   Whose top should reach unto the height of heaven;
We cannot for our lives and souls conjecture
How people raised such piles of architecture.

Show us that picture—'twould be worth the showing—
   When miracles were wrought to save mankind;
When all dry-shod, the Israelites were going
   Across the Red Sea, wall'd up by the wind;
And Pharaoh's iron chariots, and armed host,
Were madly rushing in to be o'erwhelm'd and lost.

Display that scene, when for the son of Nun
   Thou stoodest still on Gibeon, and the Moon,
At God's command, stopped over Ajalon;—
   For one whole day refused ye to go down,
While to Bethoron sped the flying Amorite,
And heaven's hailstones crush'd him in his headlong
     flight.

How many famous scenes from ancient story,
   Of Athens, Rome, and Egypt rise before me!
What monuments of art! what deeds of glory!
   "Give back the lost"—restore ye them! restore ye!
Thy pass, Thermopylæ! and, Marathon, thy fight!
Oh Sun! bring such as these, with Salamis, to sight.

But if, bright orb! the past be now denied us,
   The present time at least is in our power,
Since with thy secret, Genius hath supplied us;
   Ye pupils of Daguerre! improve the hour—
Make haste to paint the fragments which are left us,
Of what stern Time and Vandals have bereft us.

Bring us the city of great Alexander,
   Which once was so magnificent and vast;
Amid her ruins we would like to wander,
   And muse upon the glories of the past:

11*

Four thousand baths and palaces did fill her,
All crumbled into dust 'round Pompey's Pillar.

From Cairo's walls go bring that scene sublime,
  (And with our latest breath we'll bless the giver,)
Of Pyramids still battling with old Time—
  The land of Goshen and th' Eternal River!
And tomb and monument, and obelisk that stands
In solitary grandeur, 'mid the desert's sands.

Be quick, and let our eager eyes devour
  Old Hecatompylos, though not as when
Through every gate, she could at once outpour
  Two hundred chariots and ten thousand men;
But of her mighty self, the granite skeleton,
Whose giant bones for miles lie whitening* in the sun.

Imagination flags and falters on the rack—
  Description 's beggar'd, and in vain would rise
Up to thy vastness, Luxor! and Carnac!
  Naught but the eye that scene can realize—
Give us the temples! columns! gateway! propylon!-
None but thy master-hand can do it, glorious Sun!

Bring Edom's long lost Petra—she who made
  Her dwellings in the "rocky clefts"—all brought
To desolation, or in fragments laid,
  A thousand years unheard of and forgot!—
High as the eagle's nest her palaces she built,
But God did smite her for her haughtiness and guilt.

Bring us each Grecian and each Roman wreck—
  Th' Acropolis and Coliseum bring;
And Tadmor or Palmyra, and Balbec—
  The costly cities reared by Israel's king :†
Collect the whole—all left by Turk, Goth, Vandal, Hun,
In one vast gallery of pictures by the Sun.

---

  * They are neither gray nor blackened. They have no lichen
nor moss, but like the bones of man, they seem to whiten under
the sun of the desert.—*Stephens.*

  † The universal tradition of the country, according to Wood, is,
that Balbec, as well as Palmyra, was built by Solomon.

A MENTAL RETROSPECTION.

I once could see, but now am blind—
  The world is dark to me;
But, oh, 'tis fresh within my mind,
  As once it used to be.
I can recall the break of day—
  The first faint streak of light—
The mists which rose and swept away,
  Along the mountain height.
The last dim stars which 'gan to fade
  Before the approaching sun—
The flood of light his advent made—
  His glory going down.
I knew not which did please me best,—
  That flood of morning light,
Or that refulgent plunge to rest,
  Within the arms of night.

I recollect the opening Spring,
  The Violet's early bloom;
The Iris I was first to bring
  To my dear mother's room;
The Hyacinth soon followed these,
  With white or purple bells;
And shrubs among yet leafless trees
  Peep'd out from sunny dells.
The Red Bud stood, with blushes deep,
  Beside the Dogwood pale;
And made my heart exulting leap,
  Returning warmth to hail,
Methinks I now can see the wheat,
  Spread like a carpet green,
With peach and cherry blossoms sweet,
  Embroid'ring all the scene.

That wheat, in Summer, changed in hue—
  Wav'd like a sea of gold—
And as the soft winds o'er it flew,
  'Twas beauteous to behold;

Those blossoms had been early shed—
　　The type of man's own doom;
For thus as soon our early dead
　　Oft sink into the tomb.
But, oh! their place was quick supplied
　　By many a verdant leaf;
And for the loss of those who died,
　　There was no heart for grief.
For there was fruit, and there were leaves—
　　Fast flutt'ring ev'ry one—
The shady veils which Mercy waves
　　To curtain out the sun.

Autumnal days! ah, they were soft—
　　Sometimes with smoky light;
And those were sad; but then they oft
　　Foreran the clear and bright.
And then the wood—the waving wood—
　　Look'd rich beyond belief;
With some trees dyed as red as blood,
　　And some with golden leaf;
Deep orange tints, and purple too,
　　Were mix'd with evergreen,
And ev'ry shade and ev'ry hue
　　Within the rainbow seen;
In color'd map, these trees were group'd
　　All over hill and dale—
And such the groves, where fairies troop'd,
　　In some Arabian tale.

But Winter came to blast that scene,
　　And lay it bleak and bare;
And nothing save the evergreen,
　　Was left of all so fair.
How was it, glorious evergreen!
　　That thou wert smiling on,
When other trees around, were seen
　　So sad and woe-begone?
Yet, still there was in winter's face
　　A charm unto my eye;
A might—a majesty and grace,
　　To lift the soul on high:

The storm and tempest sweeping past,
  The torrents too of rain,
The flaky snows descending fast,
  And burying all the plain.

And there were moonbeams cold and bright,
  Out on the waste which froze;
What lovelier thing than starry night,
  Upon the sparkling snows?
"The floor of heaven was thick inlaid
  With patines of bright gold;"*
A firmament beneath was made—
  A mimic heaven unroll'd.
Yes, Winter, lock'd in "thick-ribb'd ice,"
  Thou too had charms for me:
Those skies were worth a countless price,
  And I could welcome thee.
Life's winter on me dreary lies,
  And dark my path on earth,
But I may see those starry skies,
  Through my Redeemer's worth.

Battle of New Orleans.

Of Jackson and the brave,
  The day to mem'ry bring,
When to battle o'er the wave,
  Came the host of England's king;
And their ships poured them out along the strand.
  Our hearts of sterling gold,
  Saw their phalanxes unfold,
  And Packenham the bold
Led the band.

* Sit Jessica: look how the floor of heaven
  Is thick inlaid with patines† of bright gold.
                    Merchant of Venice.

† Patines were small flat dishes used in the administration of the Euchanst.

In column close they form,
  As the signal rocket flew,
And on our lines to storm,
  In the deepest silence drew:
It was a winter morn, as they tell,
  When threat'ning came the crowd,
  Like a red Sirocco cloud,
  Which would wrap us in its shroud,
As it fell.

The blood within us rushed
  To meet at once the foe,
But the throbbing heart was hushed,
  To strike a deadlier blow;
Fire! at length, our captains cried, when huzza,
  Broke out upon their sight,
  A sheet of vollied light,
  As volcano was it bright,
On the air.

Huzza! huzza! huzza!
  Destruction raged around,
And our thunderbolts of war
  Scatter'd havoc o'er the ground,
And the pride of British hearts 'gan to quail;
  In anguish now they wheel,
  And in path of blood they reel,
  Yet those are hearts of steel,
Though they fail.

The carnage it is done,
  Their thousands strew the plain,
What courage could they won,
  They "quit themselves like men,"
And the laurel of the brave never dies;
  But let Old England hear us,
  If again she comes so near us,
  'Twere better far to· fear us,
Than despise.

But ere the song be ended,
  The tribute let us pay,
To him whose skill defended
  Our commonwealth that day;

A watchword be his name to the free,
　No dangers shall appal,
　Let us gather at the call,
　To conquer or to fall,
As would he.

Then loud the song be sounded,
　The storm be ever blest,
Which Britain's force confounded,
　The storm from out the West,
And Jackson be the theme of ev'ry tongue—
　Our sons shall read the story
　Of battle-field so gory,
　High in the niche of glory
'Twill be hung.

And when summoned to his rest,
　To his place in yonder skies,
Then strike the manly breast,
　Be the tear in woman's eyes ;
If home to her bosom yet be dear,
　Let her sit in sadness pale,
　And her sigh be on the gale,
　As in anguish she shall wail,
By his bier.

THE NEW HAIL COLUMBIA.

FOR THE EIGHTH OF JANUARY.

Hail Columbia! mourning land !
Hail ye brave Jacksonian band
　Who fought and bled at New Orleans,
And now the storm of war is gone,
Meet not the meed your valor won.
Let *pure elections* be our pride,
Let the *People's will* decide.
Ever mindful of that prize,
　On the glorious Eighth, arise.
　　　Firm, united let us be,
　　　Rallying round Old Hickory ;
　　　As a band of brothers join'd,
　　　Clay and Adams foes shall find.

Once more ye Patriots! rise once more
Assert the rights we lost before;
   Let no vile arts, or base intrigue,
Defeat your will—your high intent
To make our Jackson, President;
He's virtuous, wise, and firm, and just—
In heaven we place a steady trust,
That truth and justice will prevail,
And *Coalition* projects fail.
     Firm, united let us be,
     Rallying round Old Hickory;
     As a band of brothers join'd,
     Clay and Adams foes shall find.

Sound, sound the trump of fame,
And let Tennessee's lov'd name
Ring thro' the world with loud applause—
In *Glory's* niche it shall be set,
By Washington and La Fayette.
With all their skill and all their power,
He govern'd in the martial hour;
When smiling Peace check'd War's fell rage;
He sought the tranquil *Hermitage.*
     Firm, united let us be,
     Rallying round Old Hickory;
     As a band of brothers join'd,
     Clay and Adams foes shall find.

Behold our chief, like him of Rome,
Bid him like Cincinnatus come,
    To save Columbia once again—
He's strong in virtue, firm and wise,
Each shaft at him quite harmless flies.
When hope was sinking in dismay,
And clouds obscured a former day,
Thy steady soul, Old Hickory,
Resolved on death or liberty.
     Firm, united let us be,
     Rallying round Old Hickory;
     As a band of brothers join'd,
     Clay and Adams foes shall find.

Mr. Editor—We have so many great men now-a-days, and *Dinners* have become so frequent, that I should hardly think of communicating the following account of one, were it not of a character somewhat novel, and out of the common track. What a blessed country we have, when no description of greatness can pass unrewarded, and even those who have been remarkable for their dexterity in appropriating to themselves the property of others, can assemble and do honor to their chiefs.

GREAT RASCALLY DINNER.

It having been ascertained by the inmates of the State Prison or Penitentiary, that Mr. Leonidas Lightfinger, the celebrated Bank Robber, had just been committed for the crime of embezzling $40,000, the property of the Bank, a message was sent to the keeper by a committee of the most hardened villains within the walls, requesting his permission to meet their honored compeer at a Dinner, proposed to be given him in the public yard, at the expense of the prisoners generally. They offered to submit in the most quiet manner to any arrangement the keeper might make, by guards or otherwise, to prevent the possibility of any tumult or attempt at escape. At first the keeper was a good deal at a loss what answer to return, but reflecting that he was responsible only for the safe-keeping of the scoundrels, and being somewhat curious to witness so singular a spectacle, he determined to give his consent, and having taken the precaution to double his guards, the parti-colored company assembled precisely at 2 o'clock, and sat down to a Scanty Dinner, provided for the occasion. Mr. Peter Picklock, in his woollen cap, was unanimously called upon to preside, and was supported by Messrs. Burglary and Arson, as Vice-presidents. The utmost hilarity and good fellowship prevailed; the afternoon passed off in the most delightful jollification, and at the usual *lock-up* hour the whole party were severally conducted to their respective dungeons or cells, without the occurrence of a single circumstance to interrupt the general satisfaction. The following Toasts were drank with roaring applause, even greater,

if possible, than that at the Barton dinner in Ohio, or
at the Feast of Nullification in Charleston.

1st. *Our distinguished guest, Leonidas Lightfinger—*
We sympathize in his misfortunes, but glory in the
brilliancy of his achievements; his is no ordinary grasp,
he makes a sweep of forty.

A bumper.—Music, *Rogue's March.*

After the noise had subsided, Mr. Lightfinger arose,
and thus addressed the company :

FELLOW PRISONERS—With feelings of unusual emo-
tion, I rise to return my sincere thanks to this assem-
bly, which has not its parallel in the world, for the
unmerited compliment contained in your toast, and for
the very high honor you have this day conferred upon
me. It shall remain deeply laid up in my bosom, and
urge me to new exertions in our glorious cause, when
the tedious forms of an unjust incarceration, against
which I enter my solemn protest, are gone through, and
I shall again be ushered forth to the world, improved
and strengthened by the force of your example. Hunted
from society by the despicable limbs of the law, for no
greater crime than the venial attempt to distribute more
equally the blessings of the earth, improperly accumu-
lated in the hands of a few avaricious monopolists—I
find myself unexpectedly thrown into the arms of my
friends and fellow laborers in the great work of equali-
zation. Since the courtesy of our keeper permits, ought
we not to inquire for a moment, by what authority it
is, that we are thus debarred the enjoyment of glorious
liberty, the common inheritance of man ? Why it is
that they have thus shut upon us *"the windows of the
sky,"* and *"robb'd us of sweet nature's grace?"* Shall
I be told that those arbitrary enactments, called laws,
forbid the noble ends we aim at? Who, let me ask,
made those laws ?—an *aristocratical and tyrannical ma-
jority.* Have we, the minority, ever assented to these
gross usurpations of our rights? No—never, and may
"my right hand forget its cunning," if I ever do assent
to them. Has it not been recently demonstrated with a
power and eloquence never before equalled, that *majori-
ties* may oppress ? Read the debates, if you can procure

them, of the late Convention in Virginia, and the speeches delivered at the great State Rights celebration in Charleston, and say if a doubt can rest upon the subject? No, fellow prisoners, a power greater than man's has given us the right to roam at large through this vast universe, reaping where we may, and untrammelled by the odious restrictions cunningly devised by the grasping and rapacious; and since it is our unfortunate lot to live in an age, as yet unenlightened, and shackled by the chains which have been artfully forged by priests and tyrants, let us go on nobly in our design of revolutionizing the opinions of the world, and never rest until we introduce that primitive and happy state of things which existed antecedent to all law—when our first parents were left free to wander forth, with the inestimable privilege—

"Where to choose their place of rest,
    And Providence their guide."

I thank you, fellow prisoners, for the patience with which you have listened to me, and since propriety forbids me to trespass further upon your time, I will conclude with a Toast, in which I am sure of your hearty concurrence :

Miss Fanny Wright—May the dissemination of her doctrines speedily uproot the foundations of society. Drank with three times three. Music, *Black Joke.*

3d. *The Art of Stealing*—A Spartan virtue—what Lycurgus ordained, and Shakspeare practised, who can censure?

4th. *The progress of* UNCIVIL *Liberty*—as exemplified in the daily dexterity of our light-fingered gentry.

5th. *The Tariff*—That greatest of pick-pockets.

6th. *The Press*—We mean crowded theatres and plenty of pocket-books.

7th. *The renowned Barrington*—The first in—the pockets of his countrymen.

8th. *The memory of Richard Turpin*—
    He took from the rich to give to the poor,
    Oh rare Turpinaro, oh rare Dick Turpin, oh!

9th. *Jonathan Wild*—The ornament of yon—rope.

10th. *The knife which* GRINS *at the leather strap of a pair of saddle-bags.* Immense applause.

11th. *Jacob Hays*—The devil incarnate—too cunning for rogues, he must himself be the chief among them—a speedy ride for him upon the "'oss that's foaled of a hacorn,"

12th. *Petit Larceny*—The early promise of future exaltation.

13th. *Mail Bags ripped open, and contents scattered.* Music, *"Loose to the winds."*

14th. *The Pocket, the whole Pocket, and every thing in the Pocket.* Music, *"Lucy Locket's lost her pocket."*

15th. *The Destruction of the Bastile*—praised but not imitated.

16th. *Prostration to the walls of every prison in the universe, and a general Jail Delivery by the horns of some Political Joshua.*

17th. *The women in the Penitentiary*—"The world was sad." Music, *"The Campbells are coming."*

The whole party being *half shaved,* and the keeper not liking the last toast, nodded to his sentinels like imperial Jove,

> When in an instant all was still,
> And scarcely were his forces rallied,
> When out the hellish legion sallied.

TAM O'SHANTER.

THE COFFIN.

The Coffin is come! 'tis a dreadful sound!
    And tears are gushing anew,
For the family, wrapp'd in grief profound,
    Have caught that sound as it flew;
It sendeth a shock to each aching heart,
    Suspending with awe the breath;
It says that the living and dead must part,
    And seems like a second death.

Now heavy and slow is the bearers' tread,
  Ascending the winding stair,
And the steps which are echoing over head
  Awaken a deep despair;
They know by the tread of those trampling feet
  They're lifting the silent dead,
And laying him low in his winding sheet,
  In his dark and narrow bed.

Come, follow the corpse to the yawning grave—
  The train is advancing slow;
See children and friends, and the faithful slave
  In a long and solemn show—
Hark! hark! to that deep and lumbering sound
  As they lower the coffin down,
'Tis the voice of earth—of the groaning ground
  Thus welcoming back her own.

Now—ashes to ashes! and dust to dust!
  How hollow the coffin rings!
And hands are uplifted to God, the Just,
  The merciful King of kings—
"Farewell forever! Forever farewell!"
  Is heard as the crowds depart,
And the piteous accents, they seem to swell
  From a torn and broken heart.

THE OLD CHURCH.

There it stands, the old Church, on the common, alone,
  With the moss and the lichen grown gray;
Its roof is all sunken, and its doors are broke down,
And in "window'd raggedness" dark seems its frown
  On each mortal, who chanceth this way.

Like a skeleton bare, in the moon's silver ray,
  That old building stands out 'mongst the dead;
And the trav'ller in passing, stops short on his way,
Gazing up at that picture of ghastly decay—
  Whence every thing living hath fled.

12*

There was joy in heaven, and rejoicing on earth,
    When the stone of that corner was laid;
For "the wilderness bloom'd like the rose at its birth,"
And it brought the "glad tidings of peace" to each
        hearth—
    As it gather'd the flock which had stray'd.

Come enter that Ruin and stroll down its aisle,
    Let us muse on its glory o'erthrown—
See, the walls are distain'd by the scrawls of the vile,
And hands sacrilegious have plunder'd the pile—
    And its pavement with grass is o'ergrown.

Yet once, it was glorious, and its aspect was grand—
    And as smooth as the velvet, its green,
Which was trod by the great and the gay of this land,
Whose gravestones in ruins around it now stand,
    Like their spectres, still haunting the scene.

It was here that in grandeur and wealth they once roll'd;
    And that Beauty enchanted the eye,
When bedeck'd with her jewels and glitt'ring with gold,
She stepp'd from her chariot, all bright to behold,
    And her bosom with pride, beating high.

What a change since that time!—how their riches have
    flown;
    Scarce a name on their tombs can be found;
For old Time hath unchisell'd the letters of stone,
And the slabs are all green with the moss overgrown,
    And half buried they lie in the ground.

Thou art ruin'd, old Fane! yes, the arrow hath sped,
    And the iron hath enter'd indeed;
Yet thousands, yea, thousands have risen in thy stead.
Thy glory is vanish'd, but thy spirit not fled,
    For "the blood of the martyrs is seed."*

---

* The blood of the martyrs, is said to be the seed of the Church.

"I Went to Gather Flowers."

Suggested by an engraving with the above motto, representing a female who had been gathering flowers, as coming unexpectedly upon old tombstones in a wood.

"I went to gather flowers,"
　　So spake a lovely maid—
But why, amid those bowers,
　　Hangs down her drooping head?

Swift flew the laughing hours,
　　As tripp'd that gladsome maid;
Why hath she dropped her flowers?
　　Why covers she her head?

I mark what 'tis that causes
　　Her heart that sudden thrill;
I see why 'tis she pauses—
　　What thoughts her bosom fill:

Old graves are yawning on her,
　　Beneath the flow'ry sward;
Green tombstones stare upon her
　　From out an old churchyard.

A tale of dread they've told her,
　　Of beauty and its charms;
They've whisper'd Death would hold her
　　Within his mould'ring arms;

That after some bright hours—
　　And fast bright hours fly—
Some one might gather flowers
　　Where she in dust might lie.

Oh, how her teeth did chatter,
　　Oh how her frame was shook;
The tott'ring stones nod at her;
　　Look, gentle maidens, look!

Go—gather not all flowers,
　　Though they should gaily bloom;
The sweetest breathe in bowers,
　　Too near, too near the tomb.

THE TOLLING BELL.

Hark! the tolling bell!—what a fearful knell!
  How shudders the soul with dread!
'Tis the voice of death,—with his warning breath,
  He tells of the recent dead.

And where has Death been?—in the midst of kin?
  To sever the fondest ties?
Where all was so fair, has he flung despair?
  What victim in dust now lies?

Perhaps he has torn, from a heart careworn,
  Some child who had linger'd long;
And a love so pure, it shall clasp no more,
  The babe it had hush'd with song.

Perhaps he has ta'en, what had yet no stain—
  Some maid to her early tomb;
Oh! out upon Death, that his hateful breath
  Should wither her youthful bloom.

Perchance 'tis some youth, whose honor and truth
  Were plighted to her who hears;
He's shrouded to-day, and she kneels to pray,
  While bitterly fall her tears.

I know not in sooth, be it age or youth,
  'Tis an awful sound to hear,
For it makes one shrink, on the frightful brink
  To which we are all so near.

Then toll away, Bell! thine's a powerful spell
  To wake in the soul remorse;
The murderer's wrath, it may stop in its path,
  The dagger's descending force.

Aye, toll away, Bell! what better can tell
  How fleeting is all and vain,
How Death in the dark, is choosing his mark
  To add to his heaps of slain.

Toll! toll away, Death! fast fleeting's thy breath,
  Toll while thou mayest that Bell;
But strike thy last chime!—thou endest with time—
  God's trumpet shall ring thy knell.

To the Senate, on taking leave in February, 1829.

Farewell Senate Chamber, green tables and chairs,
    Farewell to the scene of my fun ;
Farewell my dear friends, I pronounce it with tears,
    My public career it is run.

No more shall I listen to speeches, sublime,
    About ev'ry thing under the sun ;   .
No more shall I sketch the discussion in rhyme,
    My public career it is run.

No more shall I grasp the warm hand of a friend,
    As here I have oftentimes done ;
Like Othello's, my business is now at an end,
    My public career it is run.

No more shall I ponder, o'er book and o'er bill ;
    Of bills I shall soon handle none ;
Like Gray, you will *"miss me some morn on the hill,"*
    My public career it is run.

I must hop over clods, with an ignoble name,
    Bid adieu to the jest and the pun ;
My Pegasus put to the plough, what a shame !
    My public career it is run.

No more shall I rummage old Commonwealth's chest,
    Or knock at her door as a dun ;
My constituents have laid my pretensions at rest,
    My public career it is run.

In my place I am told they intend to put in
    A better and worthier one ;
In the room of my *body*, you'll soon have a *Chin*,
    My public career it is run.

You have the last shot in the locker, dear friends !
    The last of a son of a gun—
My ship, d'ye see, is upon her beam ends,
    My public career it is run.

A Song for the Members of the Assembly.

TUNE.—"Meeting of the Waters."

There is not in the wide world, a city so sweet,
As the city of Richmond, where lawmakers meet:
Oh the last rays of feeling, and life must depart,
Ere the days I have spent here, shall fade from my
    heart.

Yet it is not that Cooksey, serves finest of snacks,
Good ven'son, fresh oysters, and fat canvass-backs;
It is not the sweet nectar, he gives us to swill;
Oh no, it is something more exquisite still.

'Tis that Capitol rising in grandeur on high,
Where bank notes by thousands bewitchingly lie,
Gives a charm to the scene where we figure away,
To the sweetest of tunes, sirs—four dollars a day!

Oh this spot was so sacred, our fathers loved it,
And they *writ* down enactments 'gainst serving a *writ*,
So that sheriffs and other base limbs of the law,
Must not tap here our shoulders, nor give us their jaw.

Sweet city of Richmond, how calm could I rest,
In the midst of thy mists, near the great public chest,
Where the cares which we feel in this hard world are
    lost,
While we drink and carouse, sirs, at other men's cost.

Then push round the bottle, ye lovers of fun,
Never heed here that spectre of ill, called a dun;
Should he ask his "small balance" we'll bid him to
    wait
Till we've got all the balance of funds from the state.

THE ADAMS CONVENTION.

Jackson folks! Jackson folks! all who are orthodox
  Have you heard of the great Adams meeting?—
There's a terrific squall blown in the hall,
  And you'll get a most terrible beating.

Parson Ker! parson Ker! yes he was in there—
  The State's getting fond of the Church;
This meek politician put up a petition
  That Jackson be left in the lurch.

Richmond town, Richmond town were there to look
    down
  On the things that were speaking and writing,
And some in the lobby, got up on their hobby,
  That is they went fairly to fighting.

Little Frank! little Frank! they gave the first rank,
  And the chair of the speaker he took;
But 'tis said, entre nous, he once hated John Q—,
  Think of that! think of that master Brooke!

Bob Taylor! Bob Taylor! that eloquent railer,
  Cut a splash in this Adams divan;
But if proverbs be true, no harm it will do—
  Nine tailors it takes to a man.

Ned Colston! Ned Colston! whose nick-name is roll-
    stone,
  Like Sysiphus labor'd amain;
With a very good will, he'd been working up hill,
  And was ready to do so again.

Sam Blackburn! Sam Blackburn said no man should
    backturn;
  Who once had put hand to the plough;
And his terrible eyes, he threw up to the skies,
  And shook like a lion his pow.

Chap Johnson! Chap Johnson! why he's Monsieur
    Tonson,
  Oh yes he's their Magnus Apollo!
From a whisper so small, none heard it at all,
  He gave them a Stentor-like halloo.

Now between you and I, there were many small Fry,
  Whose names 'twould be needless to mention;
What Johnson would halloo, they seem'd all to swallow,
  They came with no other intention.

What a dust! what a dust! this assembly august!
   Will raise in this ancient Dominion ;
They have in their crowns, more wisdom, by zounds!
   Than is in thy pandects, Justinian!

Jackson's gone, Jackson's gone, to all be it known—
   Let me cry like Æneas—infandum!—
They made out a ticket, and up they will stick it,
   And throw out a tub, ad captandum.

By some hocus pocus, I hope 'tis to joke us,
   Their list makes a wonderful show—
Yes, gentlemen, damn me! they've taken our Jamie,
   And followed him up with Monroe.

Rhyming lad, rhyming lad, you'll make people mad,
   You'd better be reading your Bible ;
Oh no you've forgot, 'tis adjudged, is it not,
   That truth is by no means a libel.

The Meeting of Congress.

Sound the trumpet!—beat the drum!—
To Congress come, to congress come ;
All is bustle and busy hum,
And pens are nibbing on ev'ry thumb—
     Come to the Congress, come.

All who rise to the top like scum—
All who intend to speak us dumb—
And all who mean to sit quite mum,
From ev'ry quarter, come, oh come—
     Come to the Congress, come.

Chief of the Nullifiers! Hayne!
Soil'd with dust of the southern plain,
Come once more, with your might and main,
Grapple the giant again—again—
     Come to the Congress, come.

Triton amongst the minnows small!
Spouting away upon subjects all;

Oh Daniel come to the judgment hall,
And for and against the Tariff, bawl—
        Come to the Congress, come.

Star of the South! McDuffie! come,
Shed us some light on the *"Puzzling sum,"*
Tell not in Gath, that it struck thee dumb,
But cudjel thy brains and thy noddle strum—
        Come to the Congress, come.

Men of Georgia! ho all ye
Who sigh for the land of the Cherokee,
Wirt threatens you, sirs, with a writ, we see,
But Gilmer dares him to *"Snick* and *Snee"*
        Come to the Congress, come,

Come old Tristram Shandy, come,
Hotter than hot New England rum;
Burgess thou art, and a burgess grum,
Lather away as you have done, some—
        Come to the Congress, come.

Hero of East Room memory! haste
By bloodhound Barton no longer chased,
Come with your bills of the Western Waste,
There, your affections seem wholly placed—
        Come to the Congress, com

Sons of the old Dominion! run,
The Rights of the States are all undone,
Fire your brutum fulmen gun,
'Twill make of us a figure of fun—
        Come to the Congress, cóme.

Tariff and Anti-tariff too!
Ye who the *living* Morgan slew;
Anti-masons and Workies! you
With every color and every hue—
        Come to the Congress, come.

Time would fail to summon you all
From Passamaquoddy to Anthony's fall,
From Mexico's bay to the grand canal—
Sed genus omne! the great and the small—
        Come to the Congress, come.

Bring with you, gentlemen, endless plans
To get our money and get our lands ;
The giants must lend you a hundred of hands
And Pactolus roll for you gold on the sands—
           Come to the Congress, come.

To meet them, Old Hickory ! stand to your arms
Rock of our strength! the thought of you charms—
A Veto on all which would bring on us harms!!
And a National heart which with love of thee warms!!
           Look to the Congress, look.

CANZONET TO JOHNNY.

Imitation of Canzonet to Sally.—By J. Q. ADAMS.

You, John, who have been President,
    Of these, our states united,
Should, with that glory, be content,
    Nor let your fame be blighted,
By showing still your *"frosty pow,"*
    Which *wants* a place serener,
In Congress Hall, where many a row
    Disgraces that arena.

What, though you fling your firebrand,
    By solar light or candle,
And grasp petitions in your hand,
    And many hatfuls handle,
You can but gain the poor renown,
    If you should out-debate us ;
Of burning Dian's temple down,
    Like felon Erostratus.

In Abolition's fearful path,
    You're treading on gunpowder,
And rousing up a storm, whose wrath,
    Than thunder, will be louder—
A man, more wild, was never seen
    Upon the banks of Niger,
Nor cub, more savage, bred, I ween,
    Of fierce Hyrcanian tiger.

Else wherefore was it, as they tell
    Of late, in Boston city,
That like hyena, or as fell,
    You had no tear of pity,
For Chinese folks in ing and ong,
    Eschewing opium—chewing,
But vow'd they did old England wrong
    By custom of *Koutouing*?

Old Massachusetts never bred
    An animal more rabid,
Nor one more crack'd about the head,
    Nor doing things more crabbed—
No man can tell for what you pant,
    Amid your noise and racket,—
I *guess* there's *one* thing yet you *"want,"*
    Tight-lacing in straight jacket.

Oh, place me in great Washington,
    That town, *denied to houses*,*
Where many a mighty Congress-*mon*
    Gets drunk, when he carouses.
Still shall my Muse, an humble Miss,
    Of John be always chanting,
And still the madman, Johnny, hiss,
    While *raving* and while *ranting*.

Mr. Editor.—I have felt so forcibly the moral sublimity of the scene of the Presentation of the Sword of Washington, and the Cane of Franklin, that I have made an attempt to exhibit that scene in verse. I submit it to your judgment.

THE PRESENTATION.

Say, why, in lengthen'd line,
    Hath rush'd this thronging crowd,
Up to our Hill Capitoline,
    Where flags are waving proud?

* Pone sub curru nimium propinqui,
    Solis in terra, *"domibus negata."*—Hor.

Is it in this high hall
  Some pageant to survey?
Or is some glorious festival,
  Of Freedom held to-day?

Lo! every seat is fill'd—
  Doorway and stairs are block'd,
And, now, that sea of heads is still'd,
  Which late with motion rock'd,
Why gather thus the free,
  With one consentient will?
In breathless awe, they seem to be,
  Hush'd as in death, and still.

I see an old man rise,
  And with a sword in hand,
And, glancing are a thousand eyes,
  Upon that gleaming brand.
"This is the sword" he cries,
  "Which made our people free;
No spot, nor stain, upon it lies,—
  'Twas yielded but to ye.

"This sword, historians tell,
  One hundred years ago,
Saved Braddock's army, when he fell,
  Before a savage foe.
This is the sword, whose shine,
  Our Fathers led, like star;
It is the sword of Brandywine,
  Of frozen Delaware.

"In Monmouth's sultry air,
  It did its gallant work,
And saw, amidst the cannon's glare,
  Old England yield at York.
'Twas thine, great Washington!
  And in thy valiant hand,
Like sword of God and Gideon,
  Swept Midian from our land."

A shout bursts from the throng,
  Which shakes this white-capp'd hill—
But hush!—we hear again that tongue—
  Be still!—warm hearts! be still!

"This staff to you I bring,
　　The staff of that lov'd sage,
Who snatch'd the sceptre from a king,
　　And calm'd the lightning's rage.

"On it our Franklin leau'd,
　　Whom countless thousands bless—　·
The great Philosopher—the Friend
　　Of Ploughshare and of Press.
Franklin and Washington ! ! !
　　What mighty names are here !
Will ye accept ?"—'tis done, 'tis done,
　　With one tremendous cheer.

Where should we place this sword ?
　　This staff of one so wise ?
A flaming sword, by God's high word,
　　Was placed in Paradise—
It flamed there, night and day,
　　To guard, of life the Tree,
So, let these Relics guard alway,
　　Our Tree of Liberty.

Lines Written in a Young Lady's Album.

The Prætors of Rome were accustom'd to write,
　　Their edicts of old on a table of white ;
They called it in Latin, an album, dear miss,
　　And my Anna shall issue her edicts in this—
I grant her the power of life and of death,
　　I promise to serve her as long as I've breath ;
The oath of allegiance, I take as her slave,
　　And vow I'll be hers till I sink in the grave—
What will she decree ? let it merciful be
　　The prize to be won, lovely Anna, be thee !
Go then, she replies—write a line in my book,
　　On which I may venture with patience to look ;
Ah me ! what a task for a taste so refined !
　　Where shall I the steps of true Poetry find ?

13*

Her home is in England—in Italy—Greece,—
Why will she not visit a country like this?
A thought it has struck me—perhaps 'tis a dream—
The ocean is narrowed we know to a stream,*
I'll write her a letter, and ask her to come,
And we'll give her the freedom of this Western Rome.

To Poetry.

Oh Poetry! thou nymph divine!
  Invok'd so oft in vain!
How ardently I've wished you mine—
I've wrote you many a foolish line,
But still thou let'st me inly pine,
  And die at thy disdain.

I've woo'd you in sequester'd vale,
  On side of sunny hill;
I've sought you in the moonlight pale,
When summer's sweets perfum'd the gale—
The soft pursuit did not avail,
  For thou wert cruel still.

I've sighed for you at midnight dark,
  In silence deep—profound,
I've thought I heard you coming—hark!
I said, her form I dimly mark,
She now will bring Promethean spark—
  'Twas but a cheating sound.

I've stroll'd along the sounding shore,
  Thou lov'st the path sublime;
I've climb'd the cliffs where eagles soar,
And heard the torrents deaf'ning roar,
But found thee not, nor would, I'm sure,
  Until the end of time.

In flow'ry paths, I've look'd for you,
  The beautiful, I've said
Your fancy pleased and off I flew,
Where roses round their fragrance threw,
Where earth was bright and skies were blue,
  But where wert thou, sweet maid?

*By Steam.

Why art thou cold? thou hast been kind
  To men of other climes—
The favor'd few, your haunts could find,
  You loved great Homer—Milton blind—
To Shakspeare gave the boundless mind,
  In old and bygone times.

I've often wondered how you could,
  Have such a taste, my belle!
Pope, like interrogation, stood,
  And Byron, winning all he wooed,
Would o'er his club-foot darkly brood,
  And yet you lov'd them well.

Is't country then?—this western wild,
  Dear nymph! that thou dost shun?
I thought thou lov'dst bold scen'ry child!
  The mountains upon mountains pil'd!
Primeval forests undefiled!
  Untrod since time begun.

In Avon didst thou take delight?
  Or in the "wand'ring Po?"—
What strains should then awake at sight,
  Of rivers vast, that in their flight
A thousand shores, with waters bright,
  Have wash'd?—oh! maiden show.

Yes, yes thou wilt—but not for me,
  Shalt thou awake the strain—
But here are our distinguish'd three,
  Our Bryant!—Willis!—Sigourney!—
Thy spirit stirs them, Poetry!—
  Go bid them sing again.

Oh to my country, Nymph! then come—
  Come Poetry! divine:
Here Liberty will let thee roam
  O'er all beneath her heavenly dome,
Thou could'st not find a lovelier home,
  Oh come and make it thine.

The Lowlands and the Mountains.

I stood by Calwell's fountain,
  A pilgrim at thy shrine
Hygeia! where the mountain,
  Throws round a charm divine;
And as I sadly ponder'd,
  My thoughts ran thus in rhyme,
To Home, from whence I've wander'd,
  My far off sunny clime.

The lowlands or the mountains,
  Oh! which should I love best?
Broad rivers or the fountains,
  And blue hills of the West?
Those vast and giant ranges,
  With vallies dark and deep,
Where Time hath wrought no changes,
  Or plains of boundless sweep?

The lofty hills are charming,
  And strike th' enraptur'd eye,
And *He* the heart is warming,
  Who flung them on the sky;
What shadows dark go drifting,
  Along the mountain side,
And as the clouds are shifting,
  How swiftly on they glide.

Those crowning trees! how sapless!
  Like skeletons they look,
So hoary and so hapless!
  So drear and thunder shook!
Like sentinels they're standing
  To guard some "battled tower,"
Some castle wall commanding,
  For many a weary hour.

How beautiful the white clouds,
  Upon those tops of blue!
At sunset ere the night shrouds,
  The gorgeous scene from view,

All glorious are the gildings
    Where seeming snows have roll'd,
There Fancy rears her buildings,
    Of bright and burnish'd gold.

And oh the lovely flowers,
    That deck the mountain side,
How sweet in Sylvan bowers
    They bloom in lonely pride!
The brightest there are blushing
    'Mid those of virgin snow,
And hark! how streams are rushing
    Into the vales below!

Yet more, yet more, this fountain,
    This life-inspiring spring,
Lapp'd by the blue-robed mountain,
    A holier charm doth bring—
For, here are pilgrims wending,
    Borne down by sorrow's load,
And silent prayers ascending
    Like frankincense to God.

But what are all, old Manor!
    Compared to thee, my Home!
The silver sail and banner,
    The billows lash'd to foam!
White beach and winding river!
    The Bay! the boundless Sea!—
Ah! yes, the great Lawgiver,
    Hath bound my soul to ye.

To ye, whom mem'ry mingleth,
    With boyhood's joyous plays,
Oh! how my blood it tingleth,
    To dream of those young days!
When o'er your fields I wander'd,
    Or watch'd that banner wave,
Or on that white beach ponder'd,
    Or did those billows brave.

The First Time—The Last Time.

The first time! ah what memories,
  Are mingled with that time!
What scenes—old scenes before me rise,
  To prompt the mournful rhyme.

The first time, when a careless boy,
  I sail'd my soaring kite,
How boundless was my childish joy,
  To see its cloudward flight!

The first time that I sallied forth,
  To hunt with shoulder'd gun,
What Conqu'ror issuing from the north,
  Felt prouder? Goth or Hun?—

The first time that my hand shed blood,
  As my dead bird I scann'd,
Transfix'd with horror, how I stood,
  With blood upon my hand!

Good God! if thus in boyhood,
  The blood with horror ran,
How must it curdle, when the blood
  We shed, belongs to man?

The first time that I loved!—her look,
  The light of that dark eye,
The madd'ning draughts of love I took
  Will be with me for aye.

And then the last time! oh the last!
  What bitter words are those!
They conjure up the distant past,
  And wake up buried woes.

The last time that I saw her—death
  Had closed that lustrous eye;
My lips had kissed her latest breath—
  I frantic, turned to fly.

Oh! while I touch these tender chords,
  What heart remains unwrung?
The first time and the last are words,
  On many a human tongue.

We love to muse upon them, though
  They speak of things, now lost;
The first time seems the sun's bright glow,
  The last, the killing frost.

TO MY WIFE.

You chide me oft, in softest strain.
I've heard thee often, love! complain,
  No verse I write for thee—
Come, list the reason then—'tis plain,
'Twere idle all—superfluous—vain!—
  Since man and wife are we.

Oh when we write—'tis but to tell
Some secret thoughts that inly dwell,
  And we, you know, have none,
Hath gladness made my bosom swell?
Or sorrow flung its with'ring spell?
  You've felt them in your own.

If beauty has been oft my theme,
And rapt me in extatic dream,
  Whose beauty was it?—own—
And whose the eye that shot the gleam?—
The hazle eye—the dazzling beam?
  Love!—let the truth be known.

Or if at vice, I've spurn'd, the while
And pointed to its path of guile—
  What taught me vice to fly?
What thence could all my thoughts beguile?
What but my Betsy's sunny smile?
  Thro' tears within her eye.

If virtue now has charms for me,
And all my guilty ways I flee,
  Who bade me seek my God?—
You know, my love! 'twas only thee,
His instrument thou wert for me,
  But not a chast'ning rod.

If I have sung religion's power,
Its triumph in desponding hour,
   The portrait was from life—
Though young, thy sky doth sometimes lower,
Death will the friends of all devour—
   Thou wast resign'd, my wife!

Now cast a look at every thing,
I may have sung or yet can sing;
   Your heart must throb as mine—
I know I shall not strike a string,
That will not there responsive ring,
   And wake a note of thine.

What need, my love, then write for you?
When heart to heart doth beat so true?
   You knew what I have written—
What here to others might be new,
Hath often met thy mental view,
   With joy, your soul hath smitten.

Then chide me not my angel wife,
Complain no more, my all in life,
   That lines, I write thee none—
Confess I've prov'd by reasons—rife,
I know thou art not fond of strife,
   Tho' two we are but one.

TO A BEECH TREE.

I stand beneath thee, hoary beech!
   Within this silent wood,
Where human accents seldom reach —
   But where long since, I stood
And carv'd that name, Eliza Lee,
   Upon thy yielding bark—
The letters now I dimly see,
   So time-worn is each mark.

Where are the feelings of that day ?
  Oh where my promised joy !
When passion held its madd'ning sway
  O'er me, an ardent boy ?
That name to me was like sun-light,
  As soft through clouds it broke ;
The last I murmur'd forth at night,
  The first when I awoke.

With other eyes, I look on things,
  Look on this fleeting world ;
My happiness hath taken wings,
  My hopes to earth are hurl'd—
My heart is not what it hath been,
  So chang'd it is by years
Of sorrow, sickness, death and sin,
  And unavailing tears.

But yet that name is in my heart—
  Unalter'd there it stays—
Nor can it ever thence depart,
  Like this on which I gaze—
This name, casts a damp on me,
  To see it pass away—
But why should it remain, when she
  Hath been of death the prey ?

The lost, the lov'd, the beautiful,
  The spotless and the pure—
The gentle, kind and dutiful,
  Can gladden me no more ;
But in that path, the heav'nly path,
  Trod by herself in life,
I may escape, my God, thy wrath,
  I may rejoin my wife.

THE OLDFIELD SCHOOL.

Beside yon straggling fence that skirts the way,
With blossom'd furze unprofitably gay,
There, in his noisy mansion, skill'd to rule,
The village master taught his little school.—*Goldsmith.*

When the storm of human life has passed, and the tumultuous passions have subsided into a calm, it is pleasant to look back upon the dangers we have encountered, and the narrow escapes we have had from impending destruction. Riding at anchor in the quiet haven of old age, memory loves to wander back over the past, and to contemplate the successive events by which we have been brought to our present condition. How mysteriously connected seem occurrences the most distant from one another, forming links in that long chain to which our lives may be compared! Thus seated at ease, in my old arm-chair, my snug harbor, and having recourse to that peaceful enjoyment of age, the pipe, which helps one to think, it is my purpose to recur to some incidents of my life, which illustrate the mysterious connection alluded to, and show how circumstances, the most trivial in their nature, and apparently requiring no circumspection on our parts, often give a color to our fates. With the mind's eye, I can now see the cloud, no bigger than a man's hand, which arose to spread over and darken my heavens.

Reader, I do not like my exordium; it is a style altogether unnatural to me, and savors too strongly of the circumlocutory vice of the day, to be agreeable. I shall never tell my story, if I go on in that fashion—so I pray you let me fall into my natural gait.

Well, to begin at the beginning—My parents were poor, *"but not so d——d poor, neither,"* as an old fellow once said to his lawyer, interrupting him in the midst of his speech, in which he was pathetically depicting the abject poverty of his client. Every thing depended upon the establishment of his poverty, but pride took alarm at the degrading picture, and the old man rose indignantly, and hitching up his breeches with a peculiar jerk, exclaimed, as I have said, *"not so d——d poor* *neither,"* thereby completely overthrowing the attorney whose risible muscles could no more be controlled than could those of the whole court. My parents were poor, but still they were able to educate me, as most parents then did, by sending me to an oldfield school, where the three R's, as I have somewhere read, (Reading, Riting, and 'Rithmetic,) were taught in perfection, and some Latin besides. Here I spent the morning of my existence, and while "winters of memory" are rolling over me, I look back to this school as the fountain of all the misfortunes of my life. While others recur to their school-boy days as the bright spot—the Oasis in the desert of their lives,—I see in mine nothing but the Upas tree, which blighted every thing around it. I can recall in perfect freshness the picture of our school-house and the surrounding scenery. In the centre of a large field of broom-straw, skirted on every side but one by pines, stood the house, a plain building of sawed logs, *crammed*, as we say in Virginia, with mud; on the side excepted, there was a fine grove of oaks, through which passed the public road; a common *worm* fence enclosed the yard, which was entered by a stile of rude blocks. My feelings of awe on first crossing that stile can never be forgotten. I had never seen a school-master, but had formed a dreadful idea of one, having heard so much of the *instructive jerk* of his arm. A buzzing sound proceeded from the house, which I could not understand. I approached and knocked, and as soon as the door was opened, such a scene met my eyes, and such a Babel of noise assailed my ears, that I stood for some time rooted to the spot. The master, a rough looking Irishman, dreadfully marked with the small-pox, was scuffling with an overgrown boy, who used in his defence, with no little dexterity, a rule, from one end of which hung a string and lead pencil. After a smart rap over the knuckles of the pedagogue, I heard the boy exclaim, *"I'll be bound you'll never write* Avoirdupois Weight* *again."* On two sides

* A famous copy at school, which, with "Evil communication corrupts good manners," will doubtless be remembered by many of my contemporaries.

of the room were ranged desks and benches, covered with large splotches of ink, and whittled almost to pieces, and around sat about twenty boys of all sizes. One little chubby-faced fellow, whose feet could not reach the floor, was crying out, at the very top of his voice, *b-l-a, bla,* and all the rest were spelling or reading in the most abominably loud and dissonant tones, and with that peculiar whine which a child at first considers as the distinctive characteristic of reading as opposed to talking. Some were at great *A,* little *a, r-o-n;* some at *a-bom-i-na-ble,* and some at *con-cat-e-na-tion*—and such a concatenation of abominable sounds I certainly had never heard in my life before. The instant they saw me, all save the combatants, were as still as Tam O'Shanter's witches, when he cried out *"weel done,* Cutty Sark.*"* Before I had power to move from the station I occupied, the scuffle between the boy and the school-master terminated in favor of the latter, who proved game, while the former showed the dunghill, and attempted a retreat through the door. As he approached, I started on one side to give him a free passage, but unfortunately he was not aware of my movement, and we came in contact, by which means the whole party, school-master and all, tumbled heels over head into the yard. The rebellious boy by this means was caught, and received in my presence such a *lashing,* as proved our teacher to be fully as expert as *"the most expert flogger in all Oviedo."*

Such was my initiation into the mysteries of an old-field school; and the reader will see at once, that I cannot be held responsible for the defects of my education. What could I learn in this Babel but the confusion of tongues? There reigned here a constant struggle between democracy and despotism; and notwithstanding the strong arm of authority was against us, the physical force was on our side—and so various were our means of annoying our tyrant, that he was ultimately obliged to succumb, and wink at our enormities. When I first entered this school, I was as innocent as original sin would permit me to be: I was a good boy, and said my prayers regularly, night and morning, but was soon laughed out of this; for the doctrines of infidelity had penetrated, at that time, almost every hovel in the land, and even school-boys might be heard promulgating the sentiments of the deists. I soon followed the example of those around me, and found, with Mr. Feathernest, that *"a good conscience was too expensive a luxury for me to indulge in."* I could not keep pace with my schoolmates if I remained too conscientious, and especially with Benson, the overgrown boy, who had given me my first lesson in rebellion. He was the incarnation of every thing vile, and never forgave me that unlucky tumble which I so innocently gave him on the threshhold of our school. He conceived the most inveterate antipathy to me, and left no stone unturned to thwart and vex me in every thing. So relentless' were his persecutions, that my chief study became revenge; and although obliged at first to submit to many a severe drubbing from his superior strength, I found frequent opportunities of retort, which did not leave him altogether victorious. It is not my intention to describe the multiplied incidents of such a life, which are familiar to every Virginian at least. Let it suffice, that having triumphed over our tyrant, we declared war against one another, as is often the case with more important communities, and we became divided into Bensonites and Buckskins. This feud became the all-absorbing matter of the school, and ramified itself into all our sports and occupations. Books were secondary considerations. The substitutes, positive, were boxing, jumping, leaping and bandy; the comparative, were cock-fighting and fives; the superlative, a scrub race. In all these various accomplishments I made a rapid progress—and in gaffing a cock, I became supreme. I shall not stop to enumerate my successive triumphs over Benson. I foiled him at length in every thing. Our last desperate struggle for the mastery was in a pitched battle between his game-cock, the Emperor of Germany, and my King of Prussia. The whole neighborhood assembled to witness the fight, and many were the bets upon the respective combatants. Those who have never partaken of the sport can hardly form an idea

14*

of the thrilling interest excited. In the first encounter of our royal personages, the Emperor struck the King a blow, which to all appearances seemed fatal. It was a brain stroke, and for a while my old warrior seemed paralysed : Benson was in ecstacies. Confident of the valor of his majesty, and conjecturing his situation, I sprang forward and with all the seeming odds against me, I offered to treble the bet upon the King. It was immediately taken up ; and scarcely was it done, when my veteran combatant, rousing from his temporary stupor, flew at the Emperor, and literally cut him to mince-meat. I shall take leave of my school with the acknowledgment that I issued from thence as finished a devil in most things, as Pandemonium could have turned loose; and with such exquisite accomplishments as those of cock-fighter, horse-racer and five-player, it is not wonderful that I speedily ran through the little property my well-meaning and industrious parents had made a shift to leave me. I thank God, they were spared the exhibition of my folly, by being removed from this world just as my propensities were blossoming. My reader, if I ever have one, must not, however, suppose from what I have said of my vices, that I was altogether corrupt. *"None are all evil."* I had not forgotten all the lessons of virtue I had received from my parents, and especially those which were occasionally instilled into me by a being whom I must ever revere and hold in grateful recollection : I mean the wife of my school-master, who was so meek and gentle, so kind and affectionate, such a pattern of genuine benevolence and goodness, that I loved her like a mother, and in despite of my wildness, would hearken sometimes to her counsels. She cast the bread upon the waters, and it was found afterwards in the circumstance, that although I plunged into every species of dissipation, 1 never lost that sense of honor, which kept my hands from picking and stealing, and my tongue from evil speaking, lying and slandering. I injured myself more than any one else, and I do not believe that anything could have tempted me to hurt a hair of any creature's head, Benson's excepted. Fate seemed determined to protract our warfare to the scenes of after life. We both fell in love with the same girl, and a duel would have been the consequence, had my antagonist possessed half the courage of his Emperor of Germany; but cowardice is always the associate of cold-blooded villainy. I know not whether his craven spirit decided our love affair in my favor, but this I know, that the immortal author of the Cockiad has said, with great truth, that

> Hens, like women, though the deed be cruel,
> Won't have a cock that will not fight a duel.

Having sunk, at last, the whole of my little patrimony, and finding myself sinking fast in the estimation of those who flee with "the lees of the wine cask," I resolved on removing to a distant county, and turning over a new leaf. Sated with pleasure, as it is foolishly called, and pressed by necessity, I determined to try that sort of life which had been so often recommended by my excellent friend, and by dint of industry and economy was doing well, when, as Providence ordered, my evil genius, Benson strayed to the neighborhood, and settled himself as a carpenter in our little county town. I know not whether there be any thing in the feeling which we call presentiment, but I remember a sort of sinking at my heart when this man first crossed my path. He accosted me in terms of an old acquaintance, and I did not repel his civilities; but I secretly resolved to have as little to do with him as possble, because I was fully aware of the profligacy of his nature, and I was not so secure in my own resolutions of amendment as not to fear contamination from his company. He seemed determined to force himself upon me, and notwithstanding all my efforts to shun him, I could not avoid altogether the discredit of his friendship. This was particularly disagreeable to me, because I had formed many valuable acquaintances, and depended wholly upon their good opinion for success in my business. It was not long before the peace of our village was disturbed by this serpent having made his way into our paradise. He corrupted our youths, and introduced the scenes of riot and debauchery, where all before was good order and quiet. Gambling, racing and cock-fighting were the elements which seemed necessary to his existence; and how he contrived to support the extravagance of his expenditure upon his slender means as a workman, was more than any one could tell. 1 never joined in any of his excesses, but, as I said before, I could not avoid the discredit of his acquaintance, and came in for my share of the odium which insensibly attaches itself to those who have been familiar with the worthless; and at the same time I incurred the vindictive hatred of Benson, who had never forgotten the ancient enmity of our school-boy days; and the time was rapidly approaching when he had an opportunity of glutting his malice to the fullest extent.

One morning, about day-break, in the month of February, 17—, I was crossing the country to my daily employment, in order to gain a public road, which led to the place of my occupation, when just as I struck the highway, my ear caught the rapidly retreating sounds of a horse's feet, and looking to my right I saw the figure of a horseman, just disappearing at an angle of the road. I thought the figure resembled Benson's, but the view was so transient that I might be mistaken, and I deemed this the more probable because I supposed him at that time to be in another part of the country. I proceeded down the road in an opposite direction, and had not gone more than a half mile, when I discovered near a small thicket on the side of the road, the dead body of a man, covered with blood. His hat was placed near him, with some papers and his watch in it, and a pistol was slightly grasped in his right hand. At a small distance was a horse saddled and bridled, and tied to a tree. It was impossible that the horseman should have passed without seeing these objects, and I therefore supposed that he might have entered the public road at a cross one, which I had passed before arriving at the spot. I immediately recognized the body to be that of an elderly gentleman of the neighborhood, who was somewhat singular in his manners, but he.

was rich and not known to be unhappy, or under any possible inducement to commit so desperate a deed as self-murder. Upon further examination, I picked up the half burnt wadding of the pistol, and unfolding it perceived it was a piece of calico, the figure of which was easily discernible; the propriety of its preservation, however, never occurred to me. I continued to hold it in my hand as I proceeded in my inquiries, and without thinking of it, or intending to do so, I put it in my pocket, and never thought of it again until some time after. I examined the ground, which was very hard frozen, but could perceive no other tracks than those of the horse which had belonged to the dead, and even those were scarcely to be seen. What should I do? was now the question. I concluded it would be best to mount the horse; and ride off as speedily as possible to the mansion of the old gentleman, and give the alarm to his son who resided with him; I did so, and returned with him immediately to the scene. We made no other discovery which could lead to a development of the mystery; we went to the cross-road spoken of, and saw the faint traces of a horse upon it, as I had conjectured. The young man informed me that his father had determined the previous week upon a journey to the town of ——, and probably had a considerable sum of money about him, but we could find none. His watch was a very valuable one, and would doubtless have been taken had he been murdered. The placing of his papers and his watch in his hat, looked like a deliberate design, which could scarcely be imputed to an assassin, whose hurry upon a public road would have been too great for such deliberation. The pistol, however, he had never seen before. His father had frequently manifested some slight oddity of manner, but the son had never dreamed of such a termination of his existence. Upon the whole, the matter seemed to baffle conjecture, and so it appeared on the coroner's inquest. A verdict of death by some unknown means was the result, although public opinion seemed to lean to the idea of suicide. The son, however, came to a different conclusion, but still suspicion fell upon no particular person.

Three or four months had passed away, and the whole affair seemed buried in oblivion, when one day, in the presence of Benson only, I intimated my intention of setting out the following morning for the town of ——, and he carelessly asked me if I would do him the favor to sell for him a tobacco note, which he had received in payment for some work. As I could see no sort of objection to so friendly an act, I readily assented; my reader must be informed that tobacco was at that time a sort of currency, and familiarly used in all transactions like money. I went to town, transacted my own business, sold the tobacco, and returned home and paid the proceeds to Benson. I thought no more of the matter until a few weeks after, when, to my utter astonishment, I was arrested upon the charge of having murdered the old gentleman abovementioned. My amazement was considered well feigned by his son, who assured me that the evidence against me was irresistible, and sneeringly asked me how I became possessed of his father's tobacco? The truth flashed instantly upon me, that I had been made the dupe of a designing villain, and at once I saw the peril of my situation. I replied that I had received the tobacco from Benson, and desired to be confronted with him, that I might see whether he would deny the truth of my assertion; the officer who arrested me consented, as Benson lived in the village where the jail was, and accordingly I stood before him, searching every lineament of his dark countenance with an eye of fire. Did you not give me a tobacco note to sell for you several weeks ago? No, was his sullen reply. Villain, I exclaimed, do you dare to deny it? and I sprang upon him with all the violence of a man who saw the desperation of his situation, unless he could obtain a confession. I should certainly have strangled the scoundrel with my grasp, had I not been overpowered by numbers, and dragged away to prison. My violence served but to confirm the suspicions of my persecutors, who saw in the workings of my countenance nothing but the evidence of vehement passions, capable of any atrocity. Left alone in my solitary prison, it may be well imagined how horrible was the train of my thoughts. I felt like some malefactor whose prison was on fire, and who saw no chance of escape from the irons which held him chained to the wall. What could I do? I had certainly sold the tobacco, and was known by the purchaser, and could be identified; no one had seen me receive the tobacco from Benson; nobody had seen me pay him the money on my return. That tobacco, it appeared, was part of a parcel of notes which were known to be in the possession of the old gentleman murdered, and found to be missing when his papers were examined by his son, who was his executor and heir, and who resolved to watch in silence their sale, as the clue to the assassin of his father. He had taken his measures wisely, and upon going to town some weeks after my visit to the same, he discovered that the note had been sold to a merchant, who, upon application, described the individual from whom he had bought it, and disclosed his name. Here was a chain of evidence absolutely conclusive, even if I had not been the person who discovered the body and gave the alarm. What would it avail to say that I had no such pistol as the one found near the body? It is always easy to procure materials which might lead inquiry astray. What object could I have in officiously disclosing the murder, and endeavoring to trace the murderer, as I had done, in company with the son? The answer was easy; the more effectually to mislead the judgment. How corroborative of my guilt was the circumstance that no trace of another horse was visible on the spot. It would be vain to urge that the author of the deed might have designedly passed on the other road, and have crossed to the thicket on foot, and having committed the crime, might have returned to his horse on that road. Conjectures of this sort might have availed, had there been any corroborative circumstances to do away with the damning fact of my having possession of the note; but there were none. No one had seen the horseman that morning but myself; Benson was supposed to be at a distance; nobody else was suspected. Could I refer to my character to screen

myself. It is true it had been good since my residence
in the county; but from whence did I come, and what
was my standing in the place of my nativity? I could
not hope for aid in that quarter. No, the death of a
felon was inevitable!

Such were the thoughts which occupied my mind
during the first night of my confinement! In the
morning came my wife and child to see me. It is im-
possible to convey any idea of the deep sense of degra-
dation I felt, notwithstanding my innocence at the re-
ception of my family in a jail. My angel wife saw my
pain and endeavored to soothe me by every means in
her power; she assured me that she doubted not my
innocence for a moment, and that she trusted in God
for my deliverance. My child climbed my knee and
asked me why I did not come home and what I staid
there for, and repeated a thousand endearing little cir-
cumstances connected with home, which wrung my
heart, and produced a feeling of bitterness which I had
never known before. I caressed him fondly and pro-
mised to come back, and beseeched my wife to take
him away, as I could not bear the agonizing emotions
he awakened. I preferred being alone, as I felt even
her company a restraint to me, while my mind was
occupied so intensely with the contemplation of my
situation. She wisely withdrew, but did not fail to
return each day, to offer me all the consolation in her
power, and to provide for my accommodation, of which
she saw me entirely regardless. I will not dwell upon
what may be readily imagined. Day after day passed
without the smallest ray of hope of escape from my
perilous condition. I employed counsel, but had no-
thing to say to him but the repetition of my innocence,
nor could he conscientiously offer me any prospect of
acquittal. The examining court was held, and the re-
sult was what might have been expected. I was
remanded to jail for further trial at the superior court,
and spent two dreadful months of tedious restraint,
though each day found me more composed and more
prepared to breast the shock of condemnation. I have
ever found this the case with me, that I have been

impatient under the trials of life, as long as there was a chance of avoiding them. Small matters always harassed me more than great ones, and now that I had viewed my condition in all its possible aspects, and had become satisfied that there was no escape from my toils, I fortified my mind and resolved to bear my lot with a firmness which should at least exempt me from contempt. I was sitting with my wife on the evening preceding my trial, and was once more detailing to her the circumstances attending my accidental discovery of the body of the old gentleman murdered. I was at her request, more minute than usual, as her mind was anxiously bent upon finding some clue to lead us from our labyrinth of difficulties. The circumstance of the half-burnt wadding of the pistol had until now passed entirely out of my mind, but the instant I mentioned it, she started up and exclaimed, what became of it? I told her it remained unnoticed in my pocket for a long time, but that at length I drew it forth accidentally one day and had thrown it into a drawer at home, which I described, not with any view of preservation, but simply to be rid of it. She clasped her hand and devoutly thanked God that there was yet a hope, and then solemnly addressed me thus: "My dear husband, I would not for worlds, awaken a hope in your bosom which may be disappointed. I perceive the enviable state of calmness to which you have been brought by the goodness of God, but, nevertheless, a sudden thought has occurred to me which I will not reveal to you, lest it should excite in your breast the same intensity of feeling which pervades mine at this moment. I must begone; farewell until to-morrow; I cannot return sooner." So saying, she hastened away, and I sought that repose which is so difficult in situations like mine. I did sleep, however, and strange to say, my dreams that night were all of a character the most pleasing, and my slumbers were more refreshing than those I had for some time experienced. But, oh! what were the thoughts which rushed upon my mind, when I awoke and returned to a consciousness of what was to take place that day? Those thoughts, rushing like a

15

whirlwind upon me, have left an impression which can never be effaced while memory lasts. It is true, I hastened to get the mastery of my mind again, and trampled down those thoughts for the day. I bore me up heroically; I attended the summons to court with alacrity; I walked through the gaping crowd with a firm step and manly look, and repeated the *"not guilty,"* with a clear and determined voice. All the horrible pageantry of a trial had passed; the jury were empannelled; the witnesses were sworn, and among them that son of Belial, Benson. The attorney for the commonwealth had recapitulated all the disgusting circumstances of the murder, and showed their necessary and unquestionable connexion with me; my counsel had arisen to speak, when a slight movement among the crowd behind me caused me to turn my head, and I beheld my wife making her way to the bar. She touched the elbow of my lawyer and whispered in his ear. He received something from her, and then begged the court to excuse him for a few moments. They readily consented to do so, and in that painful interval, I rose and fixed my eyes sternly upon Benson, determined to watch closely his diabolical countenance. His eye quailed beneath mine, and an evident paleness came over his cheek. What had produced it? Had he seen what was tendered by my wife, or did his guilty soul simply tremble before the keen glance of his victim? In a few moments my lawyer returned, and addressed the court with a strong appeal to their feelings of humanity. He described the great peril of the prisoner, and the difficulties under which he labored in producing proof to rebut a charge which seemed to be corroborated by such strong circumstances, and said that he trusted the court would have patience and indulge him in any effort he might make to establish the innocence of the accused. He then stated the particulars I have already related respecting the wadding of the pistol; its casual preservation, and its discovery by my wife, in the drawer in which I had left it. He exhibited it to the court, and asked at their hands the immediate arrest of the witness, Benson, and the detaining him in custody until a search could be made of his house, and that a warrant might issue for that purpose. He was willing, he said, to rest the hopes of his client upon the result of the investigation to be made, whether there was any thing in Benson's house from which the half-burnt calico could have been torn. It was staking all, he admitted, upon a desperate throw; but seeing no better chance, if the court would have patience to make the inquiry and it failed, he would at once surrender the cause and give up the prisoner to his fate. The court, of course, assented. Benson was forthwith arrested; the warrant issued, and the officers of justice went to make the search, accompanied by my wife and my legal adviser. Who shall count the ages which rolled away while that search was making? The time seemed to me an *eternity.* Hope was awakened, and I could not suppress the throbbings of my heart. The court seemed as still as death. I fancied amidst that awful stillness, that every one could hear the pulsations of my heart. I tried every means in my power to be calm, but each effort seemed to increase my agitation. I listened for the sound of returning footsteps until I thought my heart would burst with the suspension of my breath. I turned my eyes again upon my foe, and he too seemed striving in vain to be calm. He seemed uneasy and restless. What was the cause? Was he indignant under suspicion? or was he fearful of detection? I could not reason; my senses were confused by the rapid circulation of my blood. At last the sound of coming steps was heard; the blood curdled at my heart, and I should have fallen but for the cry of joy which burst forth from my wife, as she entered the court. *"It is found! it is found!"* she exclaimed, "and my husband will not die. He is innocent! he is innocent." In an old chest, covered up by a pile of lumber in Benson's shop, was found a counterpane, from whence had been torn the piece of calico, used in loading the fatal pistol. The figure corresponded precisely, and this, taken in connexion with my constant declaration, that I had received the tobacco from Benson, would have been conclusive against him, but in the same chest **was** discovered another pistol, the fellow of the one found in the hand of the murdered man. The testimony was thus so conclusive against him, that he acknowledged his guilt, and speedily suffered the penalty of his atrocious crimes.

Such were the baneful consequences which flowed from my education at an oldfield school, where the laxity of authority engendered every vice. In galloping across the country lately, it was my fortune to lose myself, and to emerge suddenly upon the very spot where once stood our school house. Not a vestige remained of it; the fine grove of oaks, beneath whose shade I had so often gambolled, were all cut down, and the broomstraw field was all washed by the rains into frightful gullies. Just so had time furrowed my cheek with the tears which had coursed them down, and I shuddered as I turned away from the scene of the contests of a Benson and a

BUCKSKIN.

TO MY MOTHER ON MY BIRTH-DAY.

At sunrise this morning I woke—
  Fifty-one years ago I was born ;
As the light on my vision first broke
  I thought of that joyful morn.

That morn they unkennell'd a fox—
  All nature seem'd ringing with glee
They ran him through marshes—o'er rocks
  And kill'd him and brought him to thee.

How little you dream't it was I
  Whom the huntsman were hunting that morn
That the spirit of Reynard so sly
  Had entered the babe you had borne.

And yet it was true—even so
  I've been hunted for many long years
My days have been wretched—what woe
  Have I felt in this valley of tears!—

Unkennell'd that morning, I cried,
  So rough was the greeting and rude,
The hellhounds of life were untied
  And the pack of misfortune pursued.

Ever since have they followed me hard
  I have doubled and foiled them long
But the peace of my life has been marr'd
  And I faint, and am hanging my tongue.

Dyspepsy, *a dog of great wind,*
  Is now very near to my throat,
And Colic comes biting behind
  At the date of this comical note.

To whom shall I turn me, and when?
  To the mother who bore me that morn—
So the fox will return to his den
  When pursued by the hound and the horn.

I turn then dear mother, to thee
  And ask your maternal advice—
Ah where shall I turn me and flee?—
  "My Son! *to the Pearl of great price.*"

MY LAST CANDLE.

A Parody on Campbell's Last Man.

All things must end that have a birth,
  A candle too must die,
Though 'tis the last we have on earth,
  And we no more can buy—
I see a vision as I sit
That makes my heart go pat-a-pit
  And feel as if 'twere sick;
I see the last of tallow mould
That e'er my candlestick shall hold
  A feeble tottering wick.

That candle gives a sickly glare
   Just light enough to scan
The skeletons of riches here
   Around me, lonely man !
Some have expired with use—my chairs
Are broken down and want repairs,
   My table's propt to stand,
My room, it has ten thousand holes,
And snow is drifting in by shoals
   For Boreas lends a hand.

Yet rousing up, I cast a look
   Of patience, on my need,
And close the pages of my book,
   I cannot see to read—
Then thus apostrophize my light
Thou flickering thing adieu—good night
   Thou 'lt soon be but a snuff
Thou 'lt see no more, the poorness here,
The total want of all good cheer,
   In truth 'tis bad enough.

Although by thee a man can see
   What genius hath enshrined,
The "arts which make fire, flood" to be
   The "vassals" of his mind,
Yet my "lone mansion's twinkling star"
I will not mourn that death should mar
   Thy whiteness in a thrice,
For here those arts are all a hum
I haven't a superabundant crumb
   To keep alive the mice.

So, let vile darkness fill the place
   Content I will not sigh,
It blots not long *"sweet nature's grace"*
   Nor *"shuts the window'd sky"*
To-morrow when bright Phœbus throws
His thousand suns across the snows
   And cheers me with his rise,
I can walk forth to lovelier scenes
Than are begemm'd for kings and queens,
   And may regale my eyes.

I'll want not then the yellow haze
　　Thou shed'st so faint by day
All earth in jewels then will blaze
　　And shame thy feeble ray—
Ten thousand times ten thousand dyes
In silv'ry robes will meet my eyes
　　And lift my soul from earth,
None but a God of wond'rous power
"Of mercy dropping like the shower,"
　　Could give such splendor birth.

My eyes are aching in this room
　　To watch thee quivering, die,
But yet a thought doth cheer the gloom
　　'Tis better you than I—
My lips that tell thy dying lot
Of melting grease all hissing hot
　　Of this at least may boast
Some other candle lights my way
Adown to death, unless the day
　　Receive my parting ghost.

Stay, light, while yet a little grease
　　Burns in thy brazen hearse
Stay but a moment if you please
　　And let me see my purse—
'Tis empty all—no—not a crown
I cannot chase a sixpence down,
　　Pshaw!—go then with a pun,
Thy fate is but the fate of Greece
Nought cheers her night of dark decease
　　But Liberty's bright Sun.

THE SPRINGS.

I want a mould in which to run my lead
　　You've read dear B— the Cantos of Don Juan
I'll take their stanza for what's in my head,
　　And sketch a picture which shall be a true one;

I'm filled with Sulphur, *white, blue, grey* and *red*,
  To drink such oceans, surely must undo one—
If, therefore, I should seem a spiteful devil
Excuse me—brimstone makes me thus uncivil.

I'm at the Springs, beyond the Alleghany,
  The burning sun is scorching us like stubble,
The dust declares the weather is not rainy
  And decent people have a world of trouble;
I'm sick of Springs all save old Hippocrene,
  That had no sulphur, but with rhymes did bubble,
Now bubbling rhymes are difficult to stop up
So take them, dearest B., just as they hop up.

We have assembled here a crowd of folks
  From bay of Mexico to Pass'maquoddy,
The welkin rings with laughter, caused by jokes,
  By julep sometimes and sometimes by toddy.
Alas! to me, all seems like one great hoax,
  A monstrous cheat imposed on every body—
But for the fashion, we should shun these waters
Ye fathers, mothers, brothers, sons and daughters!

Great men are plenty here, as well as little,
  The high and low, plebeians and patricians,
Small fry and great! "of fish a pretty kettle"—
  Here mingle Congressmen, grand politicians!
With men whose only business is to whittle—
  Here's one, long deemed the greatest of magicians,
And people whisper, that sulphureous station
Is just the place for dev'lish incantation.

'Tis time such calumnies should have an end
  It's like his sable majesty rebuking sin;
Or devil, undertaking broken legs to mend—
  The game is but the game of out and in,
To this pole-star alone, all needles tend,
  For this, all panic cries and clamorous din,
And things have lately had an end so tragical
That *"non-committal"* should expire with *"magical."*

How like a polypus, Springs multiply!—
   Sweet, Salt and White! the Blue, the Red, the Grey!
Like the weird Sisters in Macbeth, they cry
   And bid us, *"mingle, mingle while me may"*
Aye, blue spirits and grey, poor fools! we fly
   To curse our folly at no distant day,
For when returned to long abandon'd homes
In ghastly form our hideous demon comes.

But then we have such charming promenades!
   A gulf-stream, vast, in which are floating seen
Bewhisker'd fellows, and well bishop'd maids
   And withered beldames of a stately mien.
Then come old men, with bald and shining heads
   Which look like barbers' blocks alive, between—
Oh 'tis a scene it makes one smile to scan
In spite of all our sympathy with man.

God forbid that I should laugh at wrinkles,
   I am so wrinkled and so old myself,
But when your eye with rheum gets red and twinkles,
   Just lay yourself aside upon the shelf,
And think upon the straggling hair that sprinkles
   Your head, and do not for all Rothschild's pelf
Your sinciput in public thus exhibit
So like a skeleton upon a gibbet.

A word of bishops—tell me if you please
   What means the term?—my head is very thick,
A bishop's one who owns a diocese,
   In other words, he has a bishoprick.
Now prithee, what can ladies want with these?
   And wherefore stick them where we see them stick,
Much more do they resemble that high hump
A dromedary carries on his rump.

That great philosopher, my Lord Monboddo,
   Held men were monkies once, both male and female,
That they continued by decree of God, so,
   Till civ'lization *"dock'd th' estate in tail."*

The women doubtless will exclaim, oh lud no!
  But once their gowns were made with monstrous trail,
And now they show, by these enormous tumors,
That having tails is one of their fond humors.

Ah! ha! I've stumbled on the secret hidden
  In bishops, perched upon each lady's back,
Most women have, for ages, been *priest-ridden*.
  The seat of honor too is a woolsack
Their backs, by sacks, should *argal*, be bestridden
  And thus you see I've got upon the track:
Stop then, until I make a memorandum
That here's *quod erat demonstrandum.*

Do ladies think to laugh so much is pretty?
  Their faces gleam with everlasting light—
The beaux must now be either vastly witty
  Or else their stock of brains must be so slight
That blunders half convulse each screaming Kitty
  And she is forced to show her ivory white,
And throw her body into such contortions
From witnessing dull Witling's sad abortions.

Since I have mention'd women here so freely
  I'll handle now the Epigastric—
Why on such subjects should our mouths be mealy
  Why dont some *"Pulpit drum ecclesiastic"*
Send forth anathema of thund'ring peal, eh!
  Against that fashion, cruel and fantastic,
Of tightly squeezing up the poor abdomen,
Till busts are like inverted cones, in women.

A truce with gibes against the charming fair
  For, after all, they're ev'ry way, delightful—
Now for those mouths all covered up with hair
  Can any thing on earth be half so frightful?
Were I a despot they should dangle in mid air
  The running noose I would, with all my might, pull,
Or banish them to herd with bearded goats
Which wear such dirty patches on their throats.

But that which *beats bobtail* and makes one stare.
    That which all other fooleries doth bang,
Is the vile foppery of gumming down the hair
    Till youth looks grimmer than Ourang Outang—
A further proof that once, men monkies were,
    And to their *"hurdies"* next a tail will hang,
And if tis true, old maids lead apes about in hell
'Twill be but what is done, in *this* world, by a belle.

Nevertheless, there's something quite amusing
    About these Sulphur Springs, in what one sees
Eight hundred people constantly abusing
    The waters—table—servants—flies and flees;
And yet the whole affair's of their own choosing
    All swarming here, as swarms a swarm of bees—
And never was there such a set of gluttons
Devouring every year three thousand muttons.

A fellow has dyspepsia—*fui quorum,*
    (I choose to have the Latin changed to please me,)
Chotanker like, I take my morning jorum,
    And then expect, vain hope! the spring to ease me;
Next down my throat the buckwheat cakes I pour'em
    And then, of course, tremendous colics seize me,
The Doctor's called—one of Jack Hornbook's scholars—
I swallow pills—he swallows twenty dollars.

A man whose face is yellow as a pumpkin,
    For calomel has gone off with his liver,
With no more prudence than a country bumpkin
    Consumes more gravy than would make a river,
And feeds as freely as a Tony Lumpkin,
    Then straightway has an Indian sweat or shiver,
And yet by gas—the sulphurated hydrogen—
He hopes to get,—ye gods!—upon his legs agen.

A friend complained about his nervous system
    That Cassius like he *"could not sleep o'nights"*—
He hoped that Sulphur water would assist him
    And set his weak and shattered nerves to rights—

One day from his accustom'd round I miss'd him
   And went to seek in what were his delights—
I found him eating—what?—to catch his failing breath
Why opium forsooth, and looking grim as death.

Some **not** content with Alabama **Row**
   Get into *"state of sweet duplicity"*—*
That is, get wives "sae trig frae tap to toe"
   And get of ills a multiplicity—
The wives go fast—the gouty men so slow
   It gives disparity too much publicity—
These men who think themselves such strapping fellows
To me look'd laughable—much like Othellos.

Had I enough of time or letter paper
   I could extend far more these trifling sketches,
But time is passing like the mountain vapor,
   And I'm the veriest wretch, of all these wretches.
The ball room is the scene of many a caper,
   The waltz from foreign lands the devil fetches,
And these, I purposed B—, to lay before ye,
But I must stop—perhaps I do but bore ye.

These lines are strictly confidential, mind ye,
   And must not stagger through newspaper column.
To secrecy, I therefore firmly bind ye
   By *"smacking calfskin"* in a manner solemn,
For should you print, and I thereafter find ye,
   No matter how you may pretend t' extol 'em,
I'll drag you through a horsepond 'till you're muddy
Or beat you in arena, till you're bloody.

In some brief space, I mean to pass you by,
   A spectre still, and Springs no more explore;
Yes I will hie me home, content to die—
   "Not poppy nor mandragora" can cure,

---

* The facetious Nicklin enjoins all bachelors to stop in Alaba-
ma Row, but married men go on to Paradise, which is exclusively
devoted to all persons in "a state of happy *duplicity*."

Or quell the fiends within my breast that lie,
 Perchance, my health may smile on me no more—
Aye—there they are—the blue, the dismal devils!
My lake of brimstone is their place of revels.

I make no doubt, if we could trace these fountains
 We'd come at last to that infernal spot,
Deep in the bowels of these rock-clad mountains,
 Where Satan flounder'd and became so hot,
As Milton tells us in his dire recountings
 Of that most dark and diabolic plot,
When some curs'd spirits sought to storm all heaven,
And thence, ten million fathoms down, were driven.

ELECTION DAY,

A Parody on the Sleet.

To-day, to-day's election day! the day to hold the polls,
You'll find assembled on the ground a *heap* of jovial
  souls;
The folks are dress'd all in their best, the candidates
  are there
And jackasses are braying loud, and stallions neigh and
  rear.

Each nag and many a noble horse unto the fence is *hung*
And many a gall'd and sorry jade whose *"withers have
  been wrung;"*
The bobtail'd and the long tail'd and the nick tail'd too
  behold,
And here and there the constable takes one out to be
  sold.

The blood-red bay and sorrel see, and old Cornplanter's
  breed,
Pale as the steed that Death was on, as in St. John we
  read;

16

Here's ev'ry horse of ev'ry kind, the lame, the halt, the
    blind,
And ev'ry man may choose him one as it may suit his
    mind.

Old Polly in Virginia cloth, with gingerbread, looks gay
With all her four-pence-ha'-pennies, how rich is her dis-
    play!—
With cake and beer her table groans—it looks so neat
    and sweet,
It tempts the careless passer by, to stop, and drink, and
    eat.

Old Honeypod! thou favor'd tree! fast by our tavern
    door,
Long didst thou shade the roaring lads, the men who
    lived of yore—
But great as our good fathers were, of whom we're
    justly proud,
You never shaded yet such lads, as yonder motley
    crowd.

The tavern stands with open porch, and bar-room smell-
    ing strong
Of whiskey, where the sov'reigns take *the strong pull
    and the long,*"
And now and then some broken glass comes shivering
    to the ground,
They're getting high—I know it well, by that symbolic
    sound.

Some bully big, some Irishman, "from Ireland all the
    way,"
Spreads out his pond'rous arms and fists, and dares you
    to the fray ;
And as the bull shakes off the curs, that bark with
    might and main,
So shakes his weak assailants off, some great O'Shan-
    oughshane.

But time would fail to tell of all, that vast assembled
 host,
Election days can show to you, and what each man
 they cost—
The hiccup and the staggering gait!—how eloquent
 those signs!
*The bloody nose! the eye gouged out! "expunged by
 blacken'd lines."*

Ye despots of the earth come here, ye men of thousand
 thrones!
Come down awhile and look upon our sore and broken
 bones—
Ye queens, no air must *blow upon,* what volumes that
 man speaks!—
Who's got a murd'rous *blow upon* his ruddy swollen
 cheeks!—

'Tis Liberty he doats upon, no charms for him have
 crowns,
Unless they be the broken ones o'er which his stick
 resounds—
Then cast your baubles vile away, and bow as sure
 you ought,
To him who hath the glorious fight, of *rough and tum-
 ble* fought.

Yet this loud tumult soon must end, and mark me, 'tis
 well known,
That by the fate of human things, each king must quit
 his throne—
Oh cling not to your grandeur then—its penalties—its
 pains—
But free your wretched serfs and slaves, and knock off
 all their chains.

What though the night so soon must stop the tongues
 that loudly bawl,
The law will make them wag again—the law, the lord
 of all—

Election days must come again, in each revolving year,
And then will come the gingerbread, the whiskey, and
    the beer.

The sun has set behind the hills—the polls are closed,
    away,
My friend is dropp'd and *tears* are shed, our foes have
    won the day—
I too could shed some *tears*, alas! and dash to earth my
    wig,
But crying does no good you see—we'll take a parting
    swig.

THE DISCARDED.

Imitation of Byron's Ode to Napoleon.

Old man! but yesterday, gay Hope
    Held out to thee a wife,
And now, a shilling for a rope!
    To end thy hated life;
Is this the man of thousand pranks,
Who spent his time in "quips and cranks"
    And was with fun so rife?—
Since he, in old Ægean deep,
Nor man, nor boy, hath felt so cheap.

Thou fool! of weak and simple mind,
    To seek so high a prize!—
By gazing on that maid, I find
    Thou must have lost thine eyes;
Bewilder'd—madden'd—so love-sick
Thine only gift hath been a *kick*
    And scorn for all thy sighs—
Nor till that kick, couldst thou e'er guess
Thy chance was less than littleness.

Thanks for that lesson, it will prove
  To after old men, *this,*
That they can never hope for love
  From any youthful Miss;
That warning to declining age
Should teach it to walk off the stage,
  And never sigh for bliss
With lovely things of rosy lips,
And beauteous busts and glorious hips.

The wooing and the vanity
  Of winning charming wife,
That species of insanity
  To thee, the breath of life!—
The dance—the ball-room—and the whirl
Of waltzing with some giddy girl,
  A sort of dizzy strife—
All gone!—sad spirit, what must be
Thy feeling of vacuity!

Thy home is now so desolate,
  Thy house so gloomy grown,
I wonder thou canst stand a fate
  So dark as thou hast known;
Is it some yet small glimpse of hope
That with such change can calmly cope,
  Or dread of death alone?
To live despised! or die by cord!
The choice by thee, is one abhorr'd!

He who of old would rend the *oak*
  A sad example stands
Of folly,—for *oak* turn'd the joke,
  And caught him by the hands.
As tough a job you undertook,
And grim as Milo's in your look
  Caught in your silken bands—
Wild beasts ate up that man of fame,
But thou must be devour'd by shame.

Prometheus, who stole heav'nly fire,
  As thou wouldst fain have done,
Chain'd to a rock by heaven's great sire,
  Could not his sentence shun—
Thou in the madness of thy mind
To steal an angel hadst designed,
  And justly art undone—
He lived—the horrid vulture's prey,
But thou must pine thy heart away.

He who disclosed what passed above,
  The heathen gods among,
Was by that wicked rascal, Jove,
  Into some river flung—
Up to his chin the water rose,
The apples bobb'd about his nose,
  But could not reach his tongue—
That worst of ills !—"non frui re"
Thou'st felt, no doubt, far worse than he.

When she of Lesbos could not urge
  Young Phaon to her arms,
She jumped at once into the surge,
  And drown'd all love's alarms.
From some Leucate's awful steep
Canst thou not take the lover's leap,
  Which love at once disarms ?
'Twould better far despair become,
Than sitting thus alone, humdrum.

But thou !—from thy reluctant heart
  All hope of her is wrung,
And yet thou canst not hence depart
  Nor by grapevine be swung,
Thou hast been such an oaf or calf,
It is enough to make one laugh
  To see thee so unstrung—
To think that God's fair world hath been
Encumber'd by a thing so mean.

And earth hath lent her joys to him
  Who thus can be cast down,
Her bowls have fill'd up to the brim,
  His ev'ry care to drown—
Her beauteous hand hath given him all,
"His lines in pleasant places fall,"
  And yet that hideous frown!
Oh! sharper than a serpent's tooth
Is thine ingratitude—old youth!

Thy silly deeds are writ above,
  Writ with a pen of light;
Thy thoughts so late in life of love,
  And fall—thou hapless wight!—
If thou hadst died as madman dies,
Some gouty beau might yet arise
  To shame us by his sight—
But thou hast sunk in such deep gloom
That all seem grinning at thy doom.

Weigh'd in the scales, a jester's clay
  Is vile as other forms,
And when by death 'tis passed away
  It's eaten up by worms;
But yet methought a son of fun
Might some more striking thing have done
  His mettle to display—
Nor deem'd I, he could thus sink down
Like any poor clodhopping clown.

And she, thy sweetly blooming flower,
  That most transcendent maid!
What is she doing at this hour,
  In all her charms array'd?—
Doth she too smile before her glass
That thou hast been as sheer an ass
  As ever yet hath bray'd?
And dreamed that thou couldst grasp a prize
Made for a king to feast his eyes.

Then sit thou in thy sullen hall,
  And gaze upon the floor,
Then turn thine eyes up to the wall,
  Or saunter to the door—
Or trace, with thine all idle hand,
Thy loved one's name upon the sand
  And o'er the letters pore—
I would that some old son of grog
Could thee with cat-o'-nine-tails flog.

Thou small Napoleon! in thy trance
  What thoughts thy bosom rule?
While dreaming of thy "sunny France,"
  But one—"I've been a fool"—
Perchance while shedding tears alone,
Thou'lt turn, like Niobe, to stone.
  And thus at last get cool—
Now—Jaffier-like, I know it well,
"Hell's in thyself, and thou in hell."

DARKNESS.

No light, but rather darkness visible.—*Milton.*

Away with thee, Light! thou "effluence bright!"
  Make room for my ebon car,
When it wheels on its track, with hangings of black,
  I curtain the Moon and the Star:
I love to go forth, with the storms of the North,
  To follow the hurricane's sweep,
When the ships mounting high, ride up to the sky!
  Then down to the fathomless deep.

The lightning, it gleams, but I swallow its beams—
  My kingdom it cannot control,
The fire-rent cloud I enwrap in my shroud,
  And terror I strike to the soul;

I darken my scowl with the wind's loud howl,
  When God to the shipwreck'd speaks,
And his thunderings drown, as the ship goes down, ,
  Their wild and unearthly shrieks.

'Tis I who conceal the murderous steel,
  The assassin's remorseless blow,
And I come with the slain, when with gory stain
  He beck'neth his sleepless foe:
The murderer's path I beset with wrath,
  Each sound I invest with dread,
Ee'n the "cloister'd flight" of the bird of night
  Can waken the ghastly dead.

When the world I've hush'd with a face deep flush'd,
  Some youth to his mistress hies,
Then wrapp'd in my veil, with a cheek deadly pale,
  From her home and her friends she flies;
But, oh! when the scheme of her "love's young dream"
  Is marr'd by a cold disdain,
In deep solitude, with me must she brood,
  While her tears run down like rain.

When the merciless Jew, his Redeemer slew,
  And the veil of the Temple was rent,
The earth felt my power "until the ninth hour,"
  As I blacken'd the firmament;
Jerusalem shook, and the graves were forsook,
  Where the just and the sainted had lain;
With my mantle o'erspread, the disquieted dead,
  Walk'd forth 'mongst the living again.

In the sulphurous flake of hell's dim lake,
  I am "visible" 'midst the glare;
Those fires burn bright, but they shed no light*
  In the regions of dark despair;

    * A dungeon, horrible on all sides round
      As one great furnace flamed, yet from those flames
      No light·—*Milton*·

There floundering deep, the lost spirits weep
  And gnash in their lasting pains,
Doom'd by the great Sire to the penal fire,
  And bound in eternal chains.

In the voiceless tomb, till the final doom,
  I shall brood with my raven wing,
'Till the Saviour's breath shall cry unto death,
  "Oh, death! where is thy sting?"
I shall sleep with the dead, in their last cold bed,
  Where the worm is rioting free;
Till the Power to save, shall say to the grave,
  "Oh! where is thy victory?"

ANNETTE DE L'ARBRE.

The following lines were written beneath an engraving of
Annette De L'Arbre.

There she is—the poor maiden—the hapless Annette!
  Whose story my bosom hath wrung;
What a lesson! sad lesson to every coquette,
And its deep admonitions, ye should not forget,
  Ye lovely and thoughtless and young!

Annette was a beauty surpassingly fair;
  The fairest in Normandy seen;
She loved—and her lover was gone to the war,
And she gave at their parting a braid of her hair
  To gladden the heart of Eugene.

'Twas a talisman dear, which he treasur'd in fight
  Through a long and a bloody campaign;
And when he laid down on the cold ground at night,
'Twas pressed to his heart with a throb of delight
  And a prayer to behold her again.

    *   *   *   *

Time pass'd—and Eugene to the village return'd,
　The village where dwelt his Annette;
With feelings unalter'd, his bosom still burn'd,
And crown'd with the laurels his gallantry earn'd
　What ills were in store for him yet?

Ah, vain of her beauty—pursued as a belle,
　Of Normandy's peasantry, queen,
Though with softest affection her bosom did swell;
Annette would pretend to love others as well,
　And excited his jealousy keen.

Despairing and madden'd, he rushed from her sight,
　Nor linger'd to bid her adieu—
A ship under weigh, furnish'd wings for his flight;
And ere her soft slumbers were broken by light,
　To sea, in his frenzy, he flew.

The first news of her loss, which the fair one obtain'd,
　Filled now with dismay and despair,
Was a letter in which, wretched girl! was contain'd
That pledge she had given, her heart was enchain'd—
　That braid of her beautiful hair.

Wild, frantic, undone,—disregarding disguise,
　She flies to the beach of Honfleur—
She strains o'er the weltering waters her eyes,
A speck in the distance, the maiden descries;
　'Twas his ship—and she sank on the shore.

They bore her from thence, and from that fatal day
　Her spirits and cheerfulness fled—
She turn'd from her suitors, disgusted, away
From those that were happy, and those that were gay,
　And seem'd to all hope to be dead.

There was one—and but one—whom she anxiously
　　sought:
　'Twas the mother of absent Eugene;
On her, she, alas! had calamity brought—
She only, seem'd now to engross every thought—
　Over her, would she tenderly lean.

At length to that mother, intelligence came,
   That her penitent son would return ;
He confess'd himself selfish, acknowledged with shame,
His conduct to her was deserving all blame,
   And his duty he better would learn.

What joy sprung up in the heart of Annette !
   Her hands they were clasp'd with delight—
Ah ! happiness, then, was in store for her yet,
From the breast of her lover she'd banish regret
   If once she were bless'd with his sight.

The months roll'd away—and the time was at hand—
   The time when they looked for Eugene ;
Dark tempests had swept o'er the sea and the land,
And fragments of vessels were strewed on the strand,
   When his ship was announced in the Seine.

Dismasted and shatter'd she slowly advanced,
   While hundreds were thronging the shore—
Annette stood among them with pleasure entranced,
How sparkled her eyes ! how with joy they danced !
   At thought of their meeting once more.

Vain—vain was the hope !—the poor maiden they told,
   (And her heart like that ship was a wreck,)
That during the storm which had over them roll'd,
Eugene, (and her current of life it ran cold,)
   Had been washed by a wave from the deck.

She fell to the earth with a shriek of despair ;
   Her reason was shook from its throne ;
Dark—dark was the cloud which came over the fair,
And long did her malady baffle all care
   By friendship and tenderness shown.

But at last, from the couch of disease, she withdrew
   In a troubled—bewildering maze ;
Of the past she knew nothing, or seemingly knew,
Except that she prayed when the stormy winds blew,
   And loved on the waters to gaze.

And waving her kerchief, she seem'd to expect
  That some one was coming from sea;
The tears that were coursing each other uncheck'd,
Remembrance all gone that her lover was wreck'd,
  Too sadly proclaim'd it was he.

At times she would deck herself out as a bride,
  Her chamber with white would array—
Her cheek with the maidenly blush would be dyed,
And smiles take the place of her tears that were dried,
  And gayest she seem'd of the gay.

Meanwhile to the village, poor Eugene came back,
  His life had been saved on a spar;
A vessel for India, he cross'd on her track;
And thus with a spirit cast down—on the rack,
  His fortune had borne him afar.

But how shall he meet his dear injur'd Annette?
  Her reason, how shall she regain?
How know that his love is unchanged for her yet?
Ah! wait till her chamber in order is set,
  And deck'd for the bridal again.

So 'twas—and the day of the bridal came round,
  Annette sat array'd in her charms:
"*He's coming*," they cried, and she rose at the sound,
The door it flew open—her lost one was found!
  She knew him and sunk in his arms.

Peace entered her soul and her reason return'd,
  And she seem'd through the past to have dream'd.
Then let not a lesson thus bitterly learned,
Ye young and unthinking! be thoughtlessly spurn'd,
  Nor idle ye maidens be deemed.

Remember this tale of Annette and Eugene—
  Play not with the chords of the heart;
Those exquisite strings may be sundered I ween,
And seldom united again are they seen,
  When once they are forced to dispart.

17

DAN LONESOME.—Unfinished.

CANTO I.

Is it not Colinet, I lonesome see,
Leaning with folded arms against the tree?
Why in this mournful manner art thou found,
Unthankful lad, when all things smile around?—*Philips.*

Dan Lonesome was a wight of gentle blood
  As any in this western hemisphere;
It had not "crept through scoundrels since the flood,"
  And he could trace it up through many a year,
  Far as his country could her lov'd career—
No stain on it could tongue calumnious fling;
  Old heads could trace it higher—do not jeer,—
Up to the days of some old Saxon king,
But if they could—to do it were an empty thing.

His home, I wot, it nothing boots to tell,
  Save that 'twas somewhere in that Old Domain,
Which once wished monarchy, 'tis said, so well,
  She honor'd Charles, and loath'd base Cromwell's
      reign;
  Right gladly had she rear'd Charles' throne again,
And did resolve, if that might not be won,
  T' invite him hither, cross th' Atlantic main,
To hold for us, the sceptre and the crown—
Ah! well-a-day, that deed!—what mischief it had done!

Certes, the times are wondrous changed, when we
  The very name of king can scarce abide,
Since we have quaff'd thy cup, sweet Liberty!
  But let us not our ancestors deride;
  Sly Cromwell ceased his cloven foot to hide;
Gain'd were his ends, that subtle Archimage,
  And all his canting cunning laid aside,
The tyrant open stalk'd upon the stage;
The play was still the same—they had but turn'd the
      page.

How changed the features of that virgin land,
  Adorn'd by windings of innum'rous streams,
And wrought by Nature, with most lavish hand,
  And warm'd by influence of her softest beams!—
  Still smiles that land, and still with wealth it teems,
But where her palaces of sumptuous ease?
  Where now her lofty nobles and their dreams?
Her gardens—parks—her shady walks and ways?
Where all the stately doings of her royal days?

Gone, with the foolish hopes which gave them birth;
  Nipp'd in the very bud of their display;
Crush'd by the hand of Freedom, in her mirth,
  And spared the anguish of a slow decay;—
  Such Edens were not made to waste away
Beneath the griping hand of pamper'd pride;
  No—they were fashioned for a gentler sway,
That there, untrammell'd man might safely bide,
And waft her golden treasures down their glassy tide.

But what of Dan?—no misanthrope was he—
  He felt all kindness towards his fellow men;
But yet in paths alone he loved to be,
  'Mid waving woods, or on sequester'd plain,
  His joys and griefs all hid from mortal ken;
Both wealth and friends had he, and pleasant home;
  Yet more he coveted the lonely glen,
Or down some winding rivulet to roam,
Where gentle cascades left white wreaths of transient
    foam.

There would he sit, while eagerly he seann'd
  Some wild romance, with worn and dusky lid,
Of haunted priory with bloody hand,
  Or old chateau, in deepest myst'ry hid,
  Where glided ghosts, and secret pannels slid—
Then fell the curtain on this mortal vale;
  Of earth and all its shackles he was rid;
So rapt his soul by Fancy's high wrought tale:
Compared with bliss like his, all other blisses fail.

For him, these fictions had a charm divine;
   Her gallant youths were his companions dear—
He trod with them, o'er Alps and Appenines,
   Where bandit lurk'd amid the forests drear,
   And lights were seen to glance and disappear—
Soft maidens, too, whose superhuman charms
   Won every heart, were his peculiar care,
Till nobly rescued from ten thousand harms,
He saw them safely lock'd in love's triumphant arms.

Dreams of the day! oft would ye Dan invite
   On grass to lie, in summer shade, supine,
While Fancy plum'd her wing for pleasant flight,
   And bore him upward to her halls divine;
   No hope defeated, there could make him pine;
No cup untasted, from his lips be thrown;
   No light receding ever, there could shine;
But whatsoe'er of joy to mortal 's known
Arrived at, was at once, and easy, made his own.

Who does not thus at times gay castles build,
   'Yclept in air?—a name that suits them well;
For though more splendid far than works of Eld,
   More passing rare than all which ever fell,
   (Balbec's—Palmyra's—none could them excel,)
Yet in a moment, they will topple down,
   Nor leave one marble column, spared to tell
The tale of ruin, and in grandeur frown
Amid the crumbling relics of a past renown.

Such oft are standing seen, 'mid that decay
   By Goth and Vandal, most inhuman, wrought;
And Goths and Vandals still, in modern day,
   Will break irruptive on one's chosen spot,
   Though all unwelcome, and invited not;
Misfortunes—Griefs—pale Care—tormenting Debt—
   Then, Fancy! all thy revelry's forgot,
Reluctant, up from our sweet couch we get,
And homeward, frowning hied, to toil and writhe and
     fret.

But such the artist's most surprising skill,
    That, like enchantment of the olden rhyme,
'Tis but to ramble forth, where all is still,
    And wave a wand—when, in an instant's time,
    Her shining palaces will upward climb—
Not so, those works barbarians overthrew:
    None know to raise them to such heights sublime—
Lost are those arts by which they tow'ring grew,
And we but gaze to sigh—and curse the hand that slew.

Of late, by whim or fantasy impell'd,
    "A change came o'er the spirit of his dream"—
His love of solitude seem'd now dispell'd;
    Some gayer vision in his fancy teem'd;
    Perchance bright eyes had through his darkness
        beam'd:
I know not what—but forth the loiterer went;
    "Like standing pool" his sombre visage "cream'd,"
And I, who mark'd him, deem'd his mind intent
On some fixed thought, or deed, with hope and fear,
    'yblent.

To sadness prone, he, melancholy wight,
    A wand'rer—where, I only cared to know,
Sat gazing out upon wide waters bright,
    And from the Sidney watched their ceaseless flow;
    The waves were roaring round her buried prow;
Unnumbered vessels skimmed Potomac blue;
    Swift hurrying by the white beach seem'd to go;
Fast, fast behind, the trees and green hills flew,
Till Vernon's mournful walls broke on his thoughtful
    view.

Loud rang the bell—on board that flying ship,
    Full many a pilgrim hastened to her side;
Mount Vernon! broke from every joyous lip,
    And grateful hearts were swelling there with pride:
    Men from far countries with the native vied—
Oh heavens! it was a goodly sight to see;
    But chiefly Dan,'there silently we eyed
Our young Virginian gazing wistfully,
And with a filial love, Mount Vernon! upon thee.

17*

Fix'd there he stood, while strong emotions rose;
   That time-worn mansion fills his dreamy soul;
A holy awe around it virtue throws,
   And days of by-gone years before him roll;
   Trenton and Monmouth—Brandywine—the whole
Of that long war, at once was shadow'd forth,
   And rose with him, who won fair Freedom's goal;
With him, whose fame all other fame is worth—
Whose laurels drop not blood, but blessings on the
     earth.

With straining eye, the scene he dimly caught,
   As on he sped upon that sacred wave,
Which breaks on earth's most consecrated spot,
   And sighs beside a hero's hallow'd grave;
   "Boast of the good, and idol of the brave!"
Cried he, "though now within the voiceless tomb,
   Thy warning words have yet the power to save;
Still canst thou snatch us from impending doom—
Alive in grateful hearts, though laid in death's dark
     gloom.

"Yet where thy monument? methought its shaft
   Shot high, like beacon, for a guide at sea;
Methought those truths would here be telegraph'd,
   The words of thine immortal legacy,
   And sought, my country, by thy sons set free :—
And must ingratitude be still the bane
   Of commonwealths?—ye rulers! where are ye?
Arise, and wash from us so foul a stain,
Lest light, so lovely now, should in the distance wane.

"What have ye done, that great one to exalt,
   Who waked this boundless country into life?
Beyond that hill, oh shame! a petty vault
   Enshrouds the dust, with spirit once so rife,
   And rushing gallantly to battle strife;
A humble spot, untrophied and forlorn—
   What cutteth keener than the filial knife?
What taunt so bitter as our children's scorn?
I wrong my countrymen; each heart with grief is torn.

"What matters it our warrior's breast to lade
  With cumbrous pile of monumental stone,
When in his country's heart his grave is made—
  There fresh'ning still, as time is rolling on?
None need the tomb to canonize them, gone,
But such as, living, were the scourge of man,
Not friend;—such as should meet the public ban,
Though laid in marble state for foolish eyes to scan.

"Or what are pillars?—pyramids?—this earth
  Ne'er yet gave up an adamant too hard
For tooth of Time;—it may outlive the worth
  It would commemorate; yet, wise award!
  It yields at last and crumbles with the sward—
Or did some pyramid still lift its head,
  Baffling the conqu'ror, lo! desert-ward
An ally comes, the storm in Lybia bred,
Whelming in whirling sands this fortress of the dead.*

"Who now can tell what mighty king reposed
  Midway its height stupendous?—left aloft
Within his marble chamber deep enclosed,
  As if, in death, he impotently scoff'd

* Strabo, as quoted by Savary, says: "Towards the middle of
the height of one of the greatest pyramids, is a stone that may be
raised up. It shuts an oblique passage, which leads to a coffin
placed in the centre." This passage, open in our days, and
which in the time of Strabo was towards the middle of one face
of the pyramid, is at present only one hundred feet from the base;
so that the ruins of the covering of the pyramid, and of the stones
brought from within, buried by the sand, have formed a hill in
this place two hundred feet high. If even the Sphynx, though
defended by the pyramids against the northerly winds, which
bring torrents of sand from Lybia, be covered as high as thirty-
eight feet, what an immense quantity must have been heaped up
to the northward of an edifice, whose base is upwards of seven
hundred feet long. Herodotus, who saw it in the age nearest to
its foundation, when its true base was still uncovered, makes it
eight hundred feet square. Pliny says it covered the space of eight
acres. It seems an unquestionable fact that this pyramid was a
mausoleum of one of the kings of Egypt.—*Encyclopædia,* article
Pyramid.

His fellow dust;—he who alive had oft
Encrimson'd earth, and moved like dark simoom
  Upon his native land, when death had doff'd
  His bloody diadem, found there a tomb,
Forgot his pomp—his name,—and undeplored his
    doom.

"Would less than pyramid our chieftain serve?
  Less than was reared for Egypt's worthless king?
Less for the valor, never known to swerve,
  Than rose in honor of so mean a thing?—
  And whence would such gigantic structures spring?
Not from the labor of the happy free!
  Myriads of harness'd slaves were lashed to bring
That useless pile unto the height we see,
And kiss'd the hand which smote, and bent the servile
    knee.

"Oh no—we'll have no monument but one,
  Whose base is on the universal heart;
Its shaft, the plaudits of a world be won,
  Its capital, the nation's good,—the chart
  By which to point ambition to its part—
Dread Time, who blasts with his sepulchral breath,
  And soils, with touch defiled, the works of art,
Reluctant, leaves untorn a single wreath,
Which 'bleeding sire to son's safe keeping' did be-
    queath."

So thought and reason'd that impassioned wight,
  When up the dark blue vista sudden gleam'd
The Western Rome, just rising into sight—
  Our hill Capitoline far distant beam'd;
  O'er its high halls star-spangled banners stream'd,
How fair proportion'd and how chastely white,
  Thy temple, Freedom! to his vision seem'd,
In bold relief, on that commanding height,
So pure and beautiful! so grand, and yet so light!

"Can crime e'er lurk," thought Dan, "in aught so fair?
  Its virgin purity would answer, no;
Can men of blood presume to enter there?
  With hue of shame their guilty cheeks should glow:

From yonder portals let them turn and go—
Their footsteps would pollute that tasteful mound
Where rare trees blossom and the wild flowers blow:
Illustrious patriots there are pictured round;
The monuments of dauntless spirits fill that ground.

A marble cenotaph there meets the eye,
Symbolic, rising from a mimic sea,
Inscribed with those who died at Tripoli,
Men deem'd dishonor'd, if they lived not free;
Decatur, Somers, Israel, Wadsworth, ye
Would shame the wretch who trod that paradise;
Let none, with curse of Cain, in Eden be;
Oh hold it sacred to the great and wise,
Whose glorious deeds on earth are passports to the
skies."

Now full in view the scatter'd city rose—
Her sister city flashes on the skies—
Midway, the palace in the sunlight glows,
That fatal cynosure of thousand eyes!—
Ah! thither many a thoughtless footstep hies,
Crowds to that shrine, like Mecca's pilgrims, flow;
Beneath that hateful Upas, virtue dies;
Self-styled Republicans there gaping go,
To ape the fulsome scenes of Europe's courtly show.

With thoughts like these Dan's visage darker grows;—
Meanwhile the gallant steamer nears the shore;
Swift o'er her sides the rattling cordage goes,
And fast the vessel to the wharf they moor.
Forth from her ample womb the crowds now pour;
Men, women, baggage, barrows, all the gangway fill;
The shouts of hackmen rise in loud uproar—
Dan deem'd that demons were let loose from hell,
So wild—unearthly—seem'd that loud commingled yell.

But we must leave him 'midst this tempest whirl'd,
To mark his musings at some future time;
He hath but touch'd the threshhold of a world,
Where food abundant may be found for rhyme,

Unless perchance this would-be flight sublime
Shall melt the waxen pinions at my side,
    And hurl me headlong, with my feeble chime,
Like him of old, to deep Ægean tide,
When on Dedalian wings, through air he dared to glide.

~~~~~~~~~~~~~~~~~~~

Castellanus, or the Castle-Builder turned Farmer.

Mr. Editor,—It is a long time since I threw my
mite into the treasury of your book; Nugator's occupa-
tion's gone! was my ejaculation when last I wrote to
you. The same devouring element which has recently
plunged New York in misery and gloom, had just then
triumphed over much of my earthly possessions, but
over none more foolishly prized than sundry small
wares which were intended for your market. As there
was no prospect of getting Congress to extend the time
of the payment of *my bonds,* to which one would think
I was as justly entitled as the rich merchant, I had to
set to work as best I might, to repair the ravages of fire.
In the midst of saws and hammers, of bricks and mor-
tar, my ideas have been so vulgarized, that you must
not expect to see a Phœnix rise from my ashes. From
me you must never expect any thing but trifles, as my
signature portends; yet when I reflect that this world
is made up of small things as well as great, and that
the former are as essential to constitute a whole as the
latter, and that your book ought, no more than the
world, to consist altogether of the grand, but should
sometimes admit the trifling, I am encouraged to begin
again, although already scorched by more fires than
one, having encountered the fire of some of your critics.
As the mouse sets off to greater advantage the bulk of
the mammoth, the critics should rather be pleased than
otherwise, to see my wretched skeleton in contrast with
the vast proportions of some of your contributors,—but
enough.

Romances and novels made my neighbor Castellanus a castle-builder; nothing can be more dissimilar than the world he inhabits and that ideal one in which he always lived; like certain persons who shall be nameless, he has been literally *in* the world and *out* of it at the same time, and his experience therefore might justify a seeming paradox. I think it was Godwin, in his Fleetwood, who drew so beautiful a contrast between our *night* dreams and *day* dreams. Castellanus never could bear the former, attended by hag and night mare, where we are forever struggling to attain some goal, which we can never reach; he did not like to start affrighted out of sleep; to sink through chasms yawning beneath his feet;

"Nor toss on shatter'd plank far out upon some deep."

No, I have heard him exclaim, "Give me the dreams of day; let me recline upon some bank in summer's shade, supine, where fancy fits her wings for pleasant flight, and quickly ushers me into her radiant halls. No hope defeated can there make me grieve; no cup untasted from my lips be dashed; no light, receding ever, there can shine, but whatsoever there be of joy or love to mortals known, is seized at once and easily made my own." There are few persons, perhaps, who do not at some period of life, construct these gay castles, yclept in air, and well indeed is the appellation bestowed, for though more splendid far than the works of old; more passing rare than all of which we read;—Balbec's! Palmyra's!—none could excel them,—yet in a moment they will topple down, nor leave one marble column spared as if to point to the scene of desolation, and to mourn for its brethren, broken, ruined, and overthrown. Such monuments are sometimes seen standing amid that decay produced by Goths and Vandals; and Goths and Vandals still in modern times will break, *irruptive*, on the castle-builder's chosen spot—misfortunes! griefs! pale care! tormenting debt!—Then, Fancy, all thy revelry is forgotten; reluctantly from our sweet couch, we rise and homeward frowning hie to toil and writhe and fret. But such is the skill of the artist, that he has but to ramble forth where all is still, and wave his wand, when in an instant, like the enchantment of old, his shining palaces will upward climb. It is not so, alas! with those works barbarians overturned; none know how to raise them to such sublime heights, lost are those arts by which they towering rose, and we but gaze on them to sigh and curse the hands which slew them.

This practice of castle-building had been the habit o' Castellanus, from his boyhood. It gave him a strange unsocial turn, and made him shun the inmates of his father's house, He fled all company, and the pleasures which others pursue were rarely pleasures to him. One enjoyment he had which never palled. Some lonely seat beside a "wimping burn," or waterfall, where human sounds fell distantly; there with book in hand he drank in the lulling music with which such a place is fraught; there would he draw forth, unseen, some old romance, with worn and dusky lid, of "haunted priories," with bloody hand, or dark "Udolpho," with its deep mysteries, its gliding ghosts, and secret pannels. Then would fall the curtain on this mortal vale, and all its hateful realities, and his rapt soul would revel in the high wrought tale of fancy. For him these fictions had an unspeakable charm—gallant youths were his companions. He trod with them over Alps and Appenines, where banditti lurked amid the dreary forests, and lights were seen to glance and disappear. Soft maidens, too, were there, whose superhuman charms won every heart; encompassed by ten thousand dangers, he could not leave them, until he saw them safely locked in love's triumphant arms. Though a very ugly fellow, he had deceived himself into the belief that he should one day or other marry one of these delightful creatures, and had even settled that her name should be Julia, and thought he should be one of the happiest fellows upon earth; but, Mr. Editor, who do you think he now is? a clodhopper!! aye a miserable clodhopper! The owner of land and negroes!! In that one sentence, I sum up all of human

misery—and what do you think is his wife's name?
Peggy! Phœbus what a name!

"Cobblers! take warning by this cobbler's end."

Yes, ye castle-builders! look upon his undone con-
dition, and take warning. Take warning, parents, and
bring up your children to suit the sphere in which they
are to move. I shall not trouble you with the why and
the wherefore of his present condition, but suffice it to
say that such it is, and then picture to yourself the un-
told miseries he must endure when I depict to you the
sort of life he is leading, with such passions as I have
already described his ruling ones to be. *Imprimis:* there
is Peg—but I had better say as little as possible of her,
out of respect for the ladies, and out of regard for my
friend, because in truth, like "Jerry Sneak," he has not
eaten a *"bit of under crust since he was married,"* but
follow me if you please upon his farm, and let me in-
troduce to you his plagues and tormentors. Let us look
for the overseer—we shall find him if at home, which
is seldom the case, seated on a *stump,* with the symbol
of his office under his arm. There he is, you see,
mounted on his throne, lazily looking at the laborers;
working the land to death by injudicious cultivation;
extorting the last drop of vitality from it; a foe to every
species of improvement, and obstinately bent upon go-
ing on in the jog-trot of his predecessors. This is Cas-
tellanus' companion *ex necessitate.* Shades of the Or-
villes and Mortimers! pity him. What can there be in
common between them? What can they talk about?
About Evelina and Amanda?—Cottages covered with
woodbine and honeysuckle?—Landscapes and glorious
sunsets?—the warbling of birds?—Oh no, Suk and Sall,
negro cabins or pig-styes, corn fields and —— yes, they
can talk of birds, but they are blackbirds and crows, and
devil take their warbling—of sunset, but only to lament
the shortness of the days. His (the overseer's) themes
are rogues and runaways—he is eloquent upon hog-
stealing, and neither Simon Sensitive nor Timothy Testy
could recount more readily the miseries of human life,

18

His are the miseries of Geoponics. Rot—rust—weevil —fly and cutworm, haunt his imagination, and dwell upon his tongue. Castellanus would rather be a dog and bay the moon, than discuss such subjects. But my friend's delight was once in horses; it was one of the few pleasures he had. His fancy was early captivated by Alexander mounting Bucephalus; a horse gayly caparisoned and mounted by a steel clad knight, was a sight upon which his imagination feasted. The red roan charger of Marmion, at the battle of Flodden, had thrilled his every nerve.

> "Blood shot his eye—his nostril spread,
> The loose rein, dangling from his head
> Housing and saddle bloody red."

Oh what a picture! and that I should be obliged to exhibit to your view the counterfeit presentment. The ploughboys are just coming out of the stable with their master's horses going to plough. Here, sir, is Buck-e-fallus, as the negro boys call Bucephalus. There is no difficulty in mounting *him*; they have knocked out one of his eyes; he has a blind side and cannot see the shadow cast by the sun. If his spirit was ever as high as his namesake's, he has lost it now—that little ragged urchin can ride him with a grape-vine—raw-boned, spavined and wind-galled! let him pass, and let us see the next. This is Smiler! "Lucus a non lucendo." I suppose; alas! *he* never smiles—he reminds one of Irving's wall-eyed horse, looking out of the stable window on a rainy day. His look is disconsolate in the extreme; from the imperturbable gravity of his manners, you perceive he is dead to hope; melancholy has marked him for her own; bad feeding, constant toil, and a lost currycomb, have made him "what thou well mayest hate," although he once "set down" as "shapely a shank" as Burns' auld mare Maggie, ever did. Do you see that long-legged fellow, that Brobdignag, mounted upon the little mare mule? His legs almost drag the ground, and he ought in justice to *toat* (aye, sir, *toat*, a good word, an excellent word, and one upon which I mean to send you an etymological essay some of these days) the animal he bestrides. There are some singular traits about that mule *Golliver,* as the boys, by a singular misnomer, call *her.* She keeps fat, "while other nags are poor;" it is because she lives in the corn-field. She can open the stable-door by some inscrutable means, some sort of open sesame, gates are no impediments to her, and even ten rails, and a rider cannot arrest her progress. She seems to have a vow upon her never to leave the plantation ; she will go as far as the outer gate with her rider, but if he attempt to pass that boundary, his fate is sealed. He is canted most unceremoniously over her head, and made to bite the dust; that gate is her *Ultima Thule,* her ne plus ultra ; the utmost bound of her ambition. She has acquaintances enough, as Old Oliver says, and wished not to extend the circle. Her policy is Chinese, or perhaps like Rasselas, she once escaped from her happy valley, and was disappointed in the world—*"one fatal remembrance,"* perhaps casts its "bleak shade" beyond that gate. I know not in sooth, but heaven help me! what am I doing? If I go on thus, with the whole *stud* of my neighbor, and write at large upon every thing which torments him, I shall never have done. Suffice it then, that I give you a hasty, panoramic sketch of what he has to encounter in his rides over his farm. See him mounted on his little switch-tailed grey, which has the high sounding title of White Surrey, and whose tail is nearly cut off at the root by the crupper—the mane in most admired disorder, and fetlocks long and bushy. Now what does he behold? Barren fields—broken fences—gates unhinged—starving cattle—ragged sheep—and jades so galled, that they make *him* wince—hogs that eat their own pigs and devastate his crops—mares that sometimes cripple their own colts—cows on the contrary which have so much of the milk of *vaccine kindness,* that they suffer their offspring to suck after being broken to the cart—bulls even, that suck—rams, so pugnacious, that they butt his mules down, as the aforesaid Gulliver can attest, for often have I seen her knocked down as fast as she could rise—upon my life it's true Mr. Editor, and you need not add with Major Longbow, "what will you lay it's a lie?" It was amusing to see the ram, with head erect and fixed eye, moving round in a small circle, and watching his opportunity to plant his blows, and with all the pugilistic dexterity of Crib or Molyneux. I once knew my unfortunate neighbor to have a fine blooded colt, foaled in the pasture with his mules. These vicious devils had no sooner perceived that the colt was without those long ears which characterize their species, than they set to work with one accord to demolish the *monstrous* production, and in spite of the efforts of the mother, which fought with a desperation worthy of some old Roman, beset by a host of foes, succeeded in trampling to death her beautiful offspring. What a picture this is of some political zealots and envenomed critics, who no sooner perceive that a man has not *asses' ears,* like themselves, than they commence a senseless outcry against him and compass his destruction. I have somewhere read of a madman, and perhaps he was right, who when confined, protested he was not mad; that all mankind were madder than he, and that they were envious of his superior intellect, and therefore wished to put him out of the way. Castellanus goes to ride out with Cecilia, Camilla, the Children of the Abbey, or some such book in his pocket, and so engrossed is his mind with the elegance and refinement of those personages, that he can scarcely bear to go where his overseer is. He shuns him as much as Lovel did Captain Mirvan, or old Mr. Delville, Mr. Briggs. He turns with horror from the pictures of desolation around him, and hastens home to find consolation in the bosom of his heroines, not of his Peggy, for he cannot yet say, *"Non clamosa mea mulier jam percutit aures"** —and in truth that virtuous lady has a tongue, and with it can ring such a peal about the above mentioned unproductive state of things, that he had rather hear the "grating on a scrannel-reed of wretched straw;"—or, to be less poetical,

---

* Nay what's incredible, alack!
I hardly hear a woman's clack.—*Swift.*

and to come back to what he hears every day, he had rather listen to the music of his own cart-wheels, which grate so harshly and scream so loudly that they may be heard a mile off. The inevitable result of all I have told you, Mr. Editor, is, that my neighbor is actually sinking three or four per cent. upon his capital every year, and must come to beggary unless you can arouse him from his ridiculous castle-building, and novel reading. I wish you could see the style in which he moves with his *cara sposa* to church; they have *come down,* as we say, to an old gig, which cannot be quite as old as Noah's ark, because no two of the kind were ever seen in this world, and therefore could not have been preserved at the time of the deluge, although the brass mountings on the muddy and rain-stiffened harness are of so antique a fashion, that we might well suppose the ingenuity of that celebrated artificer in brass, Tubal Cain, was employed in their construction. This crazy vehicle is drawn by the overseer's horse, which is borrowed for the "nonce,"—because neither Buck-e-fallus nor Smiler, nor any of the stud are *fit to go,* and Gulliver, besides being a mule, has declined, as I have already shown, having any thing to do with our "external relations;" and furthermore, because this is the only conceivable mode in which my neighbor can obtain a return for that unlimited control which the said horse exercises over the corn in his corn-house. The contrast between the long lean figure, and rueful and cadaverous countenance of Castellanus, and the short figure resembling "the fat squab upon a Chinese fan," and the ruddy countenance of Mrs. Castellanus, is very striking;

> They sit, side by side, in the gig, sir, as solemn,
> As Marriage and Death in a newspaper column.

How they ever came together, except by the fortuitous concourse of atoms, I cannot divine, for certainly without disrespect, I may say, that however charming Mrs. Castellanus may be, she is not,

18*

A beauty ripe as harvest,
Whose skin is whiter than a swan all over,
Than silver, snow, or lilies.

Nor has she

A soft lip,
Would tempt you to eternity of kissing,
And flesh that melteth in the touch to blood.

But we may cease to wonder at their union, when
we reflect on the couples we see every day—so totally
dissimilar in taste and external appearance, that we may
almost believe with St. Pierre, that we love only those
who form a contrast to ourselves. "Love," he says,
"results only from contrasts, and the greater they are,
the more powerful is its energy. I could easily demon-
strate this by the evidence of a thousand historical facts.
It is well known, for example, to what mad excess of
passion that tall and clumsy soldier, Mark Antony,
loved and was beloved by Cleopatra; not the person
whom our sculptors represent of a tall, portly, Sabine
figure, but the Cleopatra whom historians paint as little,
lively and sprightly, carried in disguise about the streets
of Alexandria, in the night time, packed up in a parcel
of goods on the shoulders of Apollodorus, to keep an
assignation with Julius Cæsar."

TO NIAGARA.

I've stood, Niagara! on thy Table Rock,
  And gazed upon thy falls, in speechless wonder;
I've heard the deep reverberating shock
  Where plunge thy waters with the voice of thunder;
  And now although we are so far asunder,
Nor time, nor distance, can thy scenes efface—
  Still—still on thine immensity I ponder,
And watch thy billows in their madd'ning race
To that dread verge, where leap they into space.

Thou com'st upon me ever,—day and night;—
  Thy rapids, whirling—lashing—foaming—roaring,
Sweeping round Iris island in their flight,
  In their strong eddies, ev'ry thing devouring,
  Rush on my vision in the downward pouring
So furious—wild—magnificent and vast,
  They lift me, mentally, to heaven upsoaring,
To him, from whose eternal hands were cast
Those floods, so many thousand ages past.

Type of our world! thus rush we on forever
  In fierce contention, and in endless brawls,
Poor human wretches down life's rapid river
  In quick succession unto death's dark falls;
  The fearful leap the shudd'ring soul appals;
O'er the dread brink, we all must hurrying go;
  The God of heaven alone can heed our calls,
Eternity's vast chasm yawns below;—
But o'er the dark gulf the Lord hath spann'd his bow.

My footsteps track again, that lovely spot,
  Thine isle fast anchor'd 'midst the raging flood;
I muse on him, who once there cast his lot,
  And fled his fellows, in some angry mood;
  At midnight, it is told the mourner stood
Communing with thy cataract—alone—
  What were those ills o'er which he loved to brood?
What disapointments turn'd his heart to stone?
Or what the cries of conscience, thou alone couldst
    drown?

I ramble yet on that romantic path
  Trod by a countless multitude before;
From dizzying height, look down upon thy wrath,
  And gaze until I dare to gaze no more;
  Then wand'ring on along thy rock-bound shore,
I see, far off, that solitary land,
  That speck of earth, round which you madly roar,
Whereon the foot of man shall never stand,
Stayed by the terrors of thy dread command.

There 'mid the breakers, lies the old Detroit!
  What recollections rise up with her name!
Brave Barclay's ship in Erie's far famed fight,
  When Perry wrapp'd her in a sheet of flame—
  The trophy of our hero,—there—oh shame!
With sorrowing eyes, her skeleton I view'd,
  While the wild waves were howling round her
    frame—
I'll fated ship! once dyed with human blood,
Now torn to fragments, 'midst Niagara's flood.

But most I lov'd, from the Canadian shore,
  To view thy horseshoe, in the sun's soft light;
To hear thy "cavern'd echoes" round me roar,
  While sparkling showers swept past me, in their
    flight,
  For then, like "one entire chrysolite"
One half thy torrent seem'd—the rest pure white
Like piles of fleecy clouds at close of day,
  But rushing down from that stupendous height
With rainbows, gilding the rebounding spray—
Oh words!—ye are two weak—away—away.

LINES WRITTEN AT THE GRAVE OF MISS A. F. B.

I come lost Anne! from thy father's hall,
  Where once it was sweet to be,
When Anne would spring at the sprightly call
  On the foot of delight and glee.

She was not there and her playful air
  And the voice I loved were fled,
The forehead of snow—the wavy hair,
  And the soft and the sylph-like tread.

I clasped her not to my beating heart—
  The light of the hall was gone,
And now I come to this spot, apart
  To weep by her grave, alone.

Oh God! have they left thee here, sweet child!
   Deep laid in the silent tomb,
Where willows that weep and hawthorns wild
   But add to the reigning gloom?

What! thou left here in the dark, dark night
   When the air with the tempest roars?
And the heavens gleam with the lightning bright
   And the storm in a torrent pours?

What Anne! whose bed a mother once made
   And over it fondly hung?—
Sweet Anne! on a father's breast oft laid
   That breast unto madness wrung?

She whose eye was the azure heaven
   Lit up by its light divine?
Her skin the snow in its whiteness driven
   And tresses the gay sunshine?

Transition abhorr'd!—oh fearful thought?—
   But little one! who sleeps near?—
A brother beneath this grass-grown spot
   By the side of his sister dear?

Sweet babes! and have ye no parent now
   In the deep and the darksome bed?—
No pitying hand that can gladness throw
   O'er the place of the silent dead?

Oh! yes, the book of the holy one
   Hath a hope through a Saviour known
The caskets are here, but the gems are gone
   To be set by the Sardine throne.

The body sleeps till the trumpet calls—
   Lock'd then in endearing arms,
Together ascend to the jasper walls—
   The city of eternal charms.

CASTLES IN THE AIR.

A pleasing land of drowsyhead it was
  Of dreams that wave before the half-shut eye,
And of gay castles in the clouds that pass,
  Forever flushing round a summer sky.—*Thomson.*

In yonder clouds by sunset gilt,
  I, mimic castles see;
How like the castles that were built
  In air—by me, by me.

For soon they fade and pass away,
  Bereft, bright sun! of thee;
And mine, alas, how toppled they!
  Crumbling—round me, round me.

On bank reclin'd, with half shut eyes,
  I'd set my fancy free,
And by my magic wand would rise,
  Bright domes—like ye! like ye!

What wanted I with those bright domes?
  And who their queen should be?
For whom rose up those sparkling homes?
  Lov'd one!—for thee, for thee.

A king I reign'd in fairy land,
  'Midst revelry and glee,—
Who struck the sceptre from my hand
  The lov'd!—'twas she, 'twas she,

She broke the magic wand I own'd;
  Disdain'd my queen to be;
And ever since, there sits enthron'd
  Despair—in me, in me.

Rich sunsets! now, it wakes a pang—
  Deep pang, to gaze on ye—
Your gorgeousness but serves to hang
  Dark clouds—o'er me, o'er me.

The lights that lighted up my domes,
  Dark eyes that flashed on me,
Are turn'd away, and oh sweet homes!
  Farewell!—to ye, to ye.

~~~~~~~~~~~~~~~~~~~~

TO MISS W——.

This heart now so desolate, fairest!
  No coldness can chill;
Though nothing for me, love, thou carest,
  I dote on thee still.
I must not now meet thee, ah never!
  Except in the chambers of thought,
But there, I'll be meeting thee ever
  To dream of a happier lot.

Oh yes, in my inmost soul, sweetest,
  I meet thee at will,
And there while the moments fly fleetest,
  I gaze on thee still;
'Tis there I hang over and watch thee
  Till fancy transports me to bliss,
And then to my bosom, I snatch thee
  Imprinting the long fervid kiss.

But let it not anger thee, dearest,
  That such feelings thrill—
The heart thou so cruelly searest,
  For cold art thou still—
A star for my worship thou 'rt given
  To shed o'er my darkness thy ray,
Yet coldly and chastely through heaven
  Thou mov'st on thy glittering way.

In the depths of this bosom, maiden!
  Those depths which you fill,
Tho' my spirit's sorely laden
  I cling to thee still—

No power shall take thee, no lover
  Shall tear thee away from my heart,
There, light of my life, shalt thou hover
  Till death shall decree us to part.

THE DEATH OF THE RIVER.

Whilome, old Rappahannock lay
  In glorious beauty, bright
She moved adown her diamond way
To pay her tribute to the bay
  In gems of sparkling light.

Rich commerce floated on her tide,
  Loud sang her merry tars;
White sails were flapping in their pride
Or bellying o'er some vessel's side
  Beneath our stripes and stars.

Sometimes the steamer cleft her path,
  And drove the madden'd wave,
To dash on shore with thund'ring wrath
As if to whelm in turbid scath
  All things in wat'ry grave.

A track of blacken'd smoke she'd trail
  Belch'd from her iron throat;
An earthquake voice would fill the vale,
To scorn she seem'd to laugh the sail
  As far ahead she shot.

Look on the river now—'tis dead!
  In icy coffin laid—
With white sheet it is overspread,
Cold—still—all sign of motion fled,
  Like corpse in its last bed.

An air of desolation reigns
  Where all was life before,
. Like that some desert land retains
  Where vast white columns strew the plains,
    And cities stood of yore.

No living thing is now in sight,
  The birds have vanish'd long—
The wild goose took a loftier height,
And pour'd forth in his far off flight
    His plaintive note—cohong.

Cohong—cohong—that solemn throng
  Sent forth a dirge like sound,
As though in sad procession long
They chanted slow some fun'ral song,
    To warmer climates bound.

Oh River! thou again mayst flow
  With the returning spring,
Pennon and sail again mayst know,
And in thy waves, which sparkling go
    The bird may bathe his wing.

But when in icy fetters, low,
  I'm laid within my grave
This world again will never know
The wretch who wanders near thee, slow,
    And sings this idle stave.

Yet River! 'tis by wise men told
  I'll rise to grander scene
Where the great shepherd pens his fold,
And rivers run of living gold
    Through pastures bright and green.

Mr. Editor, I send you some African Notes, which
I hope will have a general circulation.

TO MASSA BOZ.

From de Driber of Stage Number One.

I heard Massa Boz of dat po piece of fun
You write for de British bout stage number one,
An' I tink I mus try to be writin' note too,
Case I was de driber dat day who dribe you.
Wid my Pill Jiddy, Pill,
Pill Jiddy, Pill Jiddy, Pill.

Dey cry you was comin—great hubbub it caus,
Bout great Massa Pickwick! de great Massa Boz!
But when fus in my presence, you come sir to stand
Den I see in a minnit you mighty small man.
Wid my Pill Jiddy, &c.

Ha! ha my fine feller! you come here to joke,
Den I say in dat wheel I'll soon put a spoke,
For I'll show you de way dat me dribe to de south
An' I'll make you to laf de wrong side ob your mouth.
Wid my Pill Jiddy, &c.

I jolt ober bridges an' bump on de poles,
And sink Massa Pickwick in many chuck holes;
Like de debil I dribe, an' mose nock out your tooth.
As you say dey sarve nigger down here at de south.
Wid my Pill Jiddy, &c.

An' so you complain dat we keep de bad road,
An' fling on de passenger water an' mud;
But de dut which you fling on us all in your Note
It is mo dan we spose sich a feller could toat,
Wid my Pill Jiddy, &c.

Dey tell me you laugh at my glub an' my hat—
But, pshuh! my sweet feller! "John dont care for dat,"
For your daddy, no doubt, ef you know who he was,
Bin war wosser dan dat I'm afeard, Massa Boz.
Wid my Pill Jiddy, &c.

At de staff of my whip you must hab a fling,
You say it was tied wid a piece o'twine string
Dat is true, an' I'll gib you one word to de wise
It was broke on de back ob a vender ob lies.
Wid my Pill Jiddy, &c.

Dat nigger you see settin dare on de fence—
Dat nigger, my massa, got heap o' hard sense;
An' he see by de twist ob my face an' my eye,
I had someting to tell him quite funny *bumbye*.
Wid my Pill Jiddy, &c.

I mus not forgit what old ooman did say,
When I gib her de cents you gib me dat day;
She say, "Hi! dis here present does look mighty small
To be sont by great gemman"—an' so dat is all.
Wid my Pill Jiddy, Pill,
Pill Jiddy, Pill Jiddy, Pill.

MY HUMBLE LOT.

Could I escape the humble lot
  To which I am consign'd—
It suits me ill—I like it not,
  "I'm cabin'd—cribb'd—confin'd,"
Who would I be?—where would I go
  For what exchange my toil?—
I swear and vow I hardly know,
  So let me think awhile.

I'd be an orator—a Clay,
   A Webster or Calhoun—
Oh no! I could not bear to say
   What I'd *unsay* so soon.
I'd be a Cæsar—or I'd be
   Napoleon, aye, Le grand!!—
What! live an exile out at sea,
   Or die by Brutus' hand?

I'd be a Sultan—a grand Turk;
   I would not, 'pon my soul!
For there again is dreadful work,
   The bowstring and the bowl—
An Autocrat, I would not be,
   With his accursed knout,
And Poland! I would set thee free,
   And turn all captives out.

Well, I'd be Louis Philippe then,
   A citizen made king—
No—Frenchmen are ferocious men,
   Assassins would upspring—
Gun barrels fixed all in a row,
   Machines infernal—yes,
That fifty balls at once will throw
   Would not suit *me*, I guess.

I'd be a congressman, oh lud!
   Why that is worse than all,
Some ruffians there who thirst for blood
   Would shoot me with a ball.
To meet a man in argument,
   The bully now disdains;
'Tis easier by a bullet sent
   To blow out all one's brains.

I'd be a President—oh worse!
   Much worse, upon my word—
I'd be as soon yon carrion corse,
   The prey of beast and bird—

The party dogs around would growl,
  The vultures flap their wings,
The beasts of prey would ceaseless howl,
  And tear my flesh to strings.

Will nothing do ? must I eschew
  All things beneath the sun ?
Oh no!—I'll tell you what I'd do,
  I'd do like Washington!
There's nothing there to make one start,
  "Room for the greatest !—room"—
No dagger for that noble heart !
  No exile for his doom!

Egyptians harnessed slaves to bring
  Their piles of cumbrous stone,
To sepulchre some worthless king
  Whose name is now unknown,
But freemen, for their godlike son,
  Point us to nobler charts ;
They tell us that their Washington
  Is coffined in their hearts.

But is it so ? and is he there ?—
  I mourn to answer—no—
His labor has been spent in air,
  His work they overthrow—
His warning voice, unheeded, falls,
  His legacy forgot,
Their brotherhood is lost in brawls,
  "Out—out, thou damned spot."

Then welcome, welcome, humble lot!
  What boots it to be great ?
I'll dig and delve this little spot,
  Contented with my fate.
All things are but inanities !
  The preacher tells us true—
Oh vanity of vanities !
  What shadows we pursue !!

Written on the Ballot Box of the Senate.

This little simple ballot box
Is in itself a paradox—
It often proves the silent grave
Of all that's good and all that's brave;
And yet from hence the brave and good
Derive their breath and life's best blood;
It takes alike unto its breast,
The low, the high, the worst, the best—
It is a fount as all must know
Whence "sweet and bitter waters flow;"
Within this little box of state
Oft lies extremes of love and hate;
Within its close and dark recess
Lie gen'rous deeds, and littleness;
Here patriot warmth and sacrifice
Meet int'rest vile and prejudice;
Revenge and malice both here live
With charity which doth forgive;
Here friends and foes unite—and mark
They stab each other in the dark,
This hole has proved to one poor Jack
Like that of curst Calcutta—black;
But yet it led another John,
In triumph on to Washington;
The road to heaven is straight, alas!
So is this hole through which they pass,
And yet to some it proves extensus
"Th' *Averni Facilis Descensus! !*"

LIFE.

Oh spring and summer time of life!
  Would I recall
Your days with disappointment rife?
  Oh no—not all—

Some few I might call back—how few!
   But even those
Brought with them as they past me flew,
   Unnumber'd woes.

Autumn of life! thou hadst a haze
   A soften'd light;
A melancholy twilight as of day's
   Approaching night;
Leaf after leaf, I saw them fall,
   Friend after friend,
Days sad as these, would I recall?
   Oh to what end?

Winter of life! thou'rt come at last
   Descending snows
Upon my head fall thick and fast
   Thick'ning like woes—
Life's landscape seems a dreary blank
   Life's fire a spark,
Time past a dream with troubles rank,
   The future dark.

What now can cheer thee, winter stern?
   Summer nor spring;
For immortality I yearn,
   And would take wing;
But through the coffin, it must come
   Must come that crown—
What have I done for it?—I'm dumb,
   Christ 'tis thine own.

'Tis thine to give, oh grant it me,
   Wretch that I am,
Unfit to lift my face to thee
   Crucified Lamb!
Oh then 'round thine eternal throne
   I'll join the choir,
Singing thy praises holy One,
   Son thou and Sire.